I HATE FUNDRAISING

NIKKI THOMAS

Publisher Information
Nikki Thomas Consulting
723 South 4th Street
Ironton, Ohio 45638

For more information or to contact the author, please email
Nikki@nikkithomasconsulting.com
or visit nikkithomasconsulting.com

ISBN 979-8-218-27918-9 (soft cover)
ISBN 979-8-218-43803-6 (eBook)

Cover design: Terry Dugan
Editorial team: John Greco, Cristina Wright, and Amy Sinnott
Interior design: Ben Wolf, Inc.
Publishing services provided by BelieversBookServices.com

First printing: 2024

Printed in the United States of America

*With gratitude, this book is dedicated to the
Bernard McDonough Foundation.*

*Your willingness to go above and beyond to help worthy
causes is a shining example of philanthropy in action.
Thank you for carrying on Bernard's legacy of compassion
and generosity. You are making a tremendous difference in our
corner of the world. On behalf of all the lives you've
touched, including my own, thank you.*

CONTENTS

INTRODUCTION

When I'm at a convention or a professional seminar—
some gathering for people who work in the development field—I always try to make the most of the
opportunity. You won't catch me staring at my phone
in between presentations. That's networking time, my
chance to make new acquaintances and catch up with
familiar faces, especially if the event is in my part of
the country.

This networking time is one of the most valuable
parts of these professional conferences. The connections I make are often the key to solving the problems
I'll inevitably run into at some point in a fundraising
campaign. Beyond that, it's always good to be
reminded that I'm not alone on this development journey; there are other people just as passionate about
their cause as I am about mine. Everyone has a story
they're living, and I want to hear how those stories are
progressing.

Over the last several years, however, I've noticed a
trend. Sometimes it feels like déjà vu. I just know I've
lived these moments more than a few times. All too

often, when I reconnect with a colleague I haven't seen in a long time, I'll discover they've left whatever nonprofit they had been working for in favor of a new one. This "moving on" has become so common that I've almost come to expect it. But it's more than just my circle of professional friends; nationally, the average tenure in any given development position is about eighteen months.[1]

Eighteen months. That's not long enough to make a sustained impact anywhere. Yet, dedicated, highly skilled men and women are jumping ship after just a year and a half. And like I said, I know a lot of these people. They're hardly the flighty type. They don't hop around because they're looking to earn more money or find an easy route up the professional ladder. Most development professionals—at least the ones I know—got into the field because they cared deeply about someone less fortunate than themselves. Sometimes, as in my case, they saw themselves in the eyes of the people they chose to serve. So, leaving a development director role isn't a small decision; it can be a gut-wrenching one.

Every situation is different. Of that, I'm certain. But the challenges that come with fundraising campaigns, event planning, and building projects can knock the wind right out of a person. Without the right plan in place—and sometimes even with a killer plan—there can be lots of anxiety and plenty of sleepless nights, and at the end of the road, burnout is waiting to meet you. It's no wonder development professionals are tempted to think the grass will be greener somewhere else.

I'm here to tell you, though, the grass is nearly the same shade everywhere. The very real obstacles and pitfalls of fundraising will not change simply because you've found a new nonprofit to pour yourself into. The inevitable and seemingly impossible challenges have led many people to hate fundraising, and they're the reason I wrote this book.

At the onset, I want to confess something to you: I once hated fundraising, and sometimes I still do. But I've discovered how to beat the burnout odds and reach my goals. I've found the secret to avoiding those sleepless nights (most of the time) and finding joy amid the job's challenges, even on the most difficult days. And I've learned to stick it out through good seasons and bad; as of the time of this writing, I've been with the same nonprofit, the Golden Girl Group Home, for more than sixteen years.

In the pages that follow, I share my story and a bit of what I've learned along the way. I offer lots of tips for navigating the toughest challenges and also the lessons I've learned from my biggest blunders. I hope you'll find practical help and encouragement for your own life in development. And hopefully, if I ever meet you at an industry conference, you'll tell me that you haven't just found a new job someplace else, but rather you decided to stick it out and keep fueling your passion. In the end, it's that passion, renewed and recharged every once in a while, that makes the journey worthwhile.

$5 *0.8 million.* That's the price tag on my latest building project. Needless to say, when I started fundraising, I had no idea I'd ever be asked to tackle anything quite so large. Then again, when I was just starting, raising just a few thousand dollars was daunting.

The truth is that fundraising isn't really about dollar amounts or strategies. It's not about making all the right connections or throwing the best events. It's not even about the worthiness of the cause. All these things play a role, of course, but fundraising is, first and foremost, about following your passion.

Without passion flowing through your veins, getting you up in the morning, and lighting a fire under your feet, even the most successful fundraising campaign can feel like drudgery. It's passion that drives everything else. In fact, I believe so strongly that passion is the fuel of fundraising that I would counsel anyone who's not passionate about their project to leave it and seek out a cause they are passionate about. In the long run, that will make all the difference.

In my case, passion is what drove me into fundraising in the first place. I didn't have to find my motivation; it was the air I breathed. Passion simply took over, and I had no choice but to find a way to fund my heart's desires. And so, I learned. I worked long hours. I made mistakes. At times, I cried. At others, I celebrated. I fell more times than I can count, but I always got back up again. Without passion, I never would have kept going.

Passion is the place where your story collides with your cause. Other people might not understand it, and you may not be able to put it into words, but it will be seen on your face. It will season the words you speak, and it will energize your movements. It's always personal and always meaningful. And it's all yours.

Before we dive into the subject of fundraising in earnest, I want to tell you about my passion. But to do that, I need to share a bit of my story with you. You'll need to know where I came from to understand how I got to the place I am now. And along the way, you'll discover where I found my passion.

My first memory is the sort of memory most people would like to forget. I was five years old, and I watched in terror as my father put his arms around my mother's throat and began to choke the life out of her. When he finally released his grip, Mom was unconscious. I thought she was dead. So, I did the only thing I knew to do: I ran to the phone and called 911.

I wish I could tell you this was an isolated incident —that it all got better from there—but that wouldn't be the truth. My childhood was filled with abuse, both witnessed and experienced. I didn't feel safe. I didn't know my worth. And I didn't know if life would ever be any different.

When I was about nine years old, my parents bought a bar in Setauket on Long Island. We lived above the bar, and I could never really escape the scene. All night long, there'd be loud music from the jukebox, drunken laughter, and bar fights. It never calmed down, so it was rare that I found any true rest. I had to grow up fast.

Most days, I would come home from school, walk through the bar, and see all the regulars nursing their addictions. My father was an alcoholic, so owning a bar didn't help with his problems. It only made them worse. He would get drunk and get violent. More times than I can count, he'd come upstairs to our apartment, bloodied and bruised from a bar fight, and we'd be terrified. We'd hide, or we'd leave the apartment for a while, just to escape his wrath. There were times I thought he might kill us if he had the opportunity. To this day, there's a scar over my left eye from a time I couldn't quite get away from him. He slammed my face into the corner of our refrigerator, and the blow left a gash, thick and bloody.

By the time I was fifteen, I'd gotten used to living a double life. At school, I blended in. I had a group of friends. I learned how to pretend I was "normal." But no one knew what my home life was like. They didn't know it was a living nightmare. When I went back to our apartment, I did what I needed to survive.

I could tell my mom was shriveling because of all the abuse. She had become numb, unable to function. She withdrew from us. That same year, Dad was admitted to a mental hospital and diagnosed with paranoid schizophrenia. I later learned he had confided in a psychiatrist that he had planned to kill all of us. Then, he would kill himself. It's no wonder Mom retreated inside of herself.

There were days she wouldn't move off the couch. She'd just lie there, not resting but not moving either. When I was home, I'd bring her a wet cloth for her forehead, something to try to bring her back to life. I'm sure she appreciated the care, but it was never enough to bring her out of her cocoon.

As for me, I did what most kids from troubled homes do: I made poor decisions. I hung out with the wrong people, looking for love wherever I could find it. I experimented with drugs, hoping to escape, if only for a few minutes. I seldom attended my high school classes, and as the year wore on, I attended them less and less. Eventually, I dropped out altogether, though it wasn't exactly my decision. The principal labeled me "a throw-away kid." I felt I had no choice. There was no place for me there, so I left. Mom was so numb she didn't quite understand what was happening. She signed me out with no protest. And just like that, I was done with school.

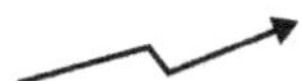

A few months after being taken out of school, I knew I needed a permanent escape. I decided to go to Boston with some friends. So, at sixteen, I was a homeless high school dropout.

Some of the friends I traveled with were deep into the punk rock scene. One of them was related to a member of the road crew for the J. Geils Band. Even though I was underage, I spent a lot of time in night clubs. The music was loud, the drugs flowed freely, and life was a bit of a blur. Now, I can look back and see all the bad decisions I made, one after another, but back then, I was just hoping to find some relief from the pain I carried with me.

When the music finally died down, we'd sleep wherever we could—usually in some cockroach-infested apartment that belonged to someone who knew someone else who knew one of my friends. During the day, I scraped by doing odd jobs.

I remember, one time, I needed money pretty badly, so I agreed to clean some woman's apartment. When I arrived, I was struck by the filth of the place. It was an absolute mess. It was hard to believe someone lived there. Sadly, the woman who hired me was just as disheveled, if not more so. It took me hours, but I cleaned and scrubbed every inch of that apartment. Toward the end, as I was straightening things up, I found a box the woman hadn't yet unpacked from her move-in sometime before. Inside were dozens of photos of a stunningly beautiful woman. They were ads for L'Oréal. I turned and asked, "Who is this woman? She's beautiful."

"That's me," she said. I was shocked. Clearly, a hard life and a drug addiction had taken its toll. I looked at her face, but I couldn't see a trace of the woman from the photographs. Then she said to me, "How do you want to get paid—in drugs or money?"

"Uh, money. Thank you."

The woman paid me, but before I could leave there was a knock at the door. She let a man in, and the two of them hurried over to the coffee table. They began freebasing cocaine right in front of me. Even though I'd been around plenty of drugs and had partaken of a few myself, I was still shocked by the display. Rather than stare, I let myself out.

Over the years that followed, I had lots of different jobs. At one point, I groomed horses at a racetrack.

Even though I had to be there at five in the morning, I loved being around the horses. There were four of them, and they were so beautiful and gentle. It felt good taking care of animals. But a racetrack can be a rough place for a young girl, and it eventually wore me down.

After that, I took a job as a cocktail waitress at a bar across from the Boston Garden. I was still underage, but I had made a friend during a short stint working at a clothing store in the city. One day, I saw one of my coworker's beautiful red Karmann Ghia, and I asked her how she had been able to afford it. She told me she worked nights as a cocktail waitress, and the tips were amazing. She could tell I was interested and that I needed the money, so she offered to get me a job there. Though I wasn't quite old enough, she assured me it wouldn't be a problem. She could vouch for me, and she just knew the owner would hire me. And that's exactly what happened.

The money I made waitressing was great. Whenever the Celtics or the Bruins were in town, the place was packed. As I got to know the bartenders, I learned how to make lots of different drinks—and I learned how to sell those drinks. The higher the tab, the higher the tips, and the more money I made. I was finally learning how to survive on my own.

But that was just it—I was surviving. I was doing what I needed to do to earn money. I wasn't thriving. I wasn't discovering who I was or anything about my potential. I had escaped my home life. I had escaped homelessness. But I hadn't arrived anywhere. At least not yet.

One night, I was hanging out with friends—the same friends with whom I'd traveled to Boston. As I mentioned, one of those friends was related to someone in the road crew for the J. Geils Band. At the time, a J. Geils Band show was a big production, and there were lots of people involved. So, I got to know quite a few people connected to the band.

Christie was one of those people. She was the fiancée of the lighting designer for the band. I don't know why, but Christie took a special interest in me. Maybe she could tell I wasn't quite old enough to be on my own. Maybe I had the look of a runaway. Whatever it was, she began asking me lots of questions. When she found out I wasn't in school, she perked up. She was finishing her degree in education and was on her way to becoming a schoolteacher, so she knew a thing or two about tutoring troubled students. Not that I was a student anymore; I had given up.

Christie didn't see it that way though. She knew I could turn things around, get my GED, and go to college if I wanted. At first, I was skeptical. But Christie believed in me. She explained how the test worked and offered to help me. Soon after, she invited me into her life. She gave me the GED prep book, and I studied it every spare moment I had. But I kept it out of sight while I was cocktail waitressing; I didn't want anyone to figure out that I was underage. For months Christie tutored me for the big test, and she mentored me. She became a big sister. For the first time in a long time, I found someone I could trust, and she set me on a path I never would have dreamed possible.

After I passed the GED, Christie encouraged me to continue my education. I attended junior college in Boston, then transferred to Johnson and Wales University, where I earned an associate's degree. Years later, after getting married, I completed a bachelor's degree in education, and I went on to earn a master's degree in theology from Kentucky Christian University. It was all possible because a stranger saw my need and decided to help.

No matter how long I live, I'll never forget Christie's kindness or the feeling of receiving my first A on a college paper. I'll also never forget that my life could've turned out very differently. With the abuse I experienced, my poor choices, and the dangers that come with homelessness and drug use, I could've ended up somewhere very different from where I am today.

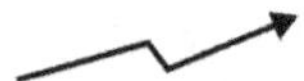

While my life post-homelessness was not without its challenges, I'm thankful for the healing that came. Sometimes it came slowly, and other times it came in leaps and bounds. Often, I would walk through long valleys of depression and anxiety before discovering a brief respite at the top of a mountain. Although, as anyone who's ever traveled along a similar path knows, the mountaintops rarely last long. The road to healing certainly wasn't a level trek.

The greatest healing in my life came when I discovered the love of God—or rather when his love reached out and took hold of me. You see, my sister-in-law's brother is a pastor, and he planted a church in Ashland, Kentucky, just a few miles from where my husband and I live in Ohio. Of course, he invited us to attend his little storefront church as he began holding services. I went, reluctantly at first. I wasn't sure what to expect from religious people. But to my surprise, they welcomed me. Even though I wore depression on my sleeve, and it was obvious I didn't have it all together, they welcomed me without conditions or judgments. I continued attending services and listened as the Bible was taught and the gospel was shared. Before long, I understood, in the deep recesses of my heart, that God loves me.

The love I'd longed for but could never find was there in Jesus's outstretched arms. It changed me from the inside out, answering the questions my soul had been asking for years. In that love, I found rest and peace, a purpose and a place to belong. Suddenly, I had a new beginning—one I never thought possible.[1]

Once I knew—really knew—I was loved by God, I was free to love others in a way I simply wasn't before. I wanted everyone to experience what I had experienced. I especially wanted people who doubted their worth to know they are more valuable in God's sight than they could imagine. Because of what I had walked through, my heart was tender toward troubled young people.

In those early days after becoming a Christian, I would drive around and see teenagers hanging out on the streets. I could see myself in some of them; they were there on the streets because home wasn't safe. They drank and used drugs because any escape from life promised relief from their pain. These were tough kids, and I knew what it was to be a tough kid. These were teenagers who didn't get invited to church, so that's what I did. I asked them if they'd like to come to church with me—and many of them said yes.

Sometimes there would be so many kids that I'd have to make multiple trips to get them all there. Before long, our little storefront church had about a dozen adults and eighty teenagers. It was quite the sight!

I'll never forget one boy named Chris. He was just thirteen years old, but, believe me when I tell you, he was the kind of kid who could fry your last nerve. He was rude and outspoken, rebellious at every turn, but I loved him unconditionally. He had more problems than most kids his age, and he had spent time in a mental hospital trying to deal with them. I was by his side throughout that season. I wanted him to know he wasn't alone.

One time, he came to church with me for a Sunday evening service. The pastor was preaching on the story of David and Goliath, and he asked Chris to come up front and hold the slingshot he had brought as a prop. I thought to myself, *Oh no! Of all the kids here tonight, Chris is the last one I would give a slingshot to!* But to my relief, the pastor didn't wind up like Goliath, and the demonstration ended without bloodshed.

Maybe it was being called up on stage, or maybe it was something in the message that night—I'm not sure —but when the service was coming to a close and the altar call was given, Chris went forward. I'm not exaggerating when I tell you his face was glowing. He was transformed in that moment. His problems weren't erased, of course, but I could see he had discovered the same love and peace I had. I smiled through my tears; I was so happy for him.

But later that night, I received a devastating phone call. Sometime after church, Chris had gotten into a car with a friend who had been drinking. There was an accident, and Chris was killed on impact. In an instant, my thirteen-year-old friend's troubled life on this earth was over. I do not doubt that as Chris passed from this life into the next, he was embraced by the love of God

—the same love he experienced that night during the service. And I do not doubt that one day, when I leave this world, Chris will be among the first to greet me in eternity.

I'm sharing Chris's story with you because it illustrates something very important about passion. Whatever you're passionate about will flow out of you in both big and small ways. I was (and still am) passionate about reaching at-risk teenagers. The world didn't take notice when a young woman from Ohio invited street teens to church, but it made a difference—not just for Chris but for all the other teenagers who were inspired to find the same hope he had found.

Fundraising and development are one channel to funnel your passion, and if done faithfully and strategically, it can have a tremendous impact for generations. It's more than raising money; it's giving life to your passion. In many cases—like mine—it's redeeming the darkest seasons of life by turning them into something beautiful for the good of those who can't fight for themselves.

Several years after we lost Chris, I stumbled into my first fundraising challenge. My troubled life as an abuse survivor and homeless teenager had a soundtrack. Punk rock had spoken to me in my angst, not necessarily drawing me out of the darkness but giving voice to my frustrations and anger. It also helped me and my friends to party, which always promised an escape from my problems—at least for a little while.

But when I became a Christian, that music no longer spoke to me, and I discovered other music, performed by bands and artists who sang about hope and the love of God. This music reminded me of what was true, even when I couldn't see it with my natural eyes. I wanted this music to minister to others, and I found myself dreaming about a huge concert festival in our community. I imagined getting some of the top Christian artists at the time to come to our community to minister to the youth. I wanted to reach out to every group home in the area and bring troubled teenagers to hear this music of hope. Mostly, I wanted those kids to encounter God.

As I dreamed, I started to put the pieces together to figure out what the event could look like. I thought of a park in downtown Ashland, Kentucky, that would be perfect for the concert. But when I tried to get a permit, I was denied. A lot of people might have given up at that point, but I was running on pure passion, so I decided I simply needed to push harder. I met with the mayor and members of the city council, and, eventually, I convinced them to let me use the riverfront. They also donated emergency services for the event—ambulances at the ready and police security. With that big win, I was ready to tackle whatever came next. And to be honest, I didn't know what came next, as I had never organized a concert before.

The first thing I needed was a headliner. I perused a Christian magazine and found a band that seemed to be advertised all the time. They weren't nationally recognized yet, so I thought I could get them to come play for us. I contacted the band's management company and booked them. I didn't have the money to cover that expense, but at least I had a starting goal.

Once I started digging in, I found out there were a lot of expenses to cover—more than I had anticipated. So, I did what any passionate person would do: I pounded the pavement. I talked with local business owners and told them about the concert. I told them about the at-risk youth in our area, shared stories of changed lives, and explained how the concert was a way to give something back to the community. As it turned out, a lot of other people wanted to give back too. I found some businesses that wanted to donate money and others that wanted to lend resources. Lots of churches chipped in as well.

As the weeks and months passed, I collected everything we would need for the big day, and I booked several local bands to fill out the rest of the roster. As a bonus, I sold enough tickets to break even. It seemed everything would go off without a hitch.

But then, the night before the concert, I received a phone call from the headlining band's manager. He was calling to tell me there was a problem. Their production director, the person responsible for all the sound equipment, was in jail! He wouldn't be able to make the show, and I needed to find my own equipment or the band couldn't go on.

Immediately, the adrenaline kicked in, and I got to work. While a lot of people might have retreated in despair, the passion coursing through me would not allow me to give up. I got a list of everything we needed from the band's manager, and first thing in the morning, I visited our local music store to get it all.

I remember asking to speak to the owner of the store, and I began rifling through my list. I had no idea how I would pay for it, but that didn't matter at the moment; I just needed to get it, or we wouldn't have a concert. The owner asked what I needed all the equipment for. He must have heard the passion in my voice, or seen the stark determination in my eyes—or a combination of the two—because he did something I'll never forget. He walked over to the speakers I needed and ripped off the tags. He said I could use them—and everything else on my list—free of charge. Apparently, passion is contagious.

That first YouthFest hosted approximately three hundred people. Though it was relatively small, it was a success, and, more importantly, I learned how to stage an event. Through trial and error, that little concert grew year after year, and by the end of its seven-year run, we averaged four thousand in attendance and hosted Grammy-winning recording artists. YouthFest left its mark on the community and impacted thousands of teenagers.

Passion is the foundation for all good work but especially fundraising. Without it, it's easy to give up when challenges arise and the going gets tough. But when passion is ignited, you can see through the problems to the success on the other side, and that success —whether it's a successful event, a new building, or meeting your organization's budget for the next fiscal year—makes it all worth it.

I realize that when I say passion needs to be the driving force behind fundraising, there will be some people who believe a passion for fundraising—by its own merit—is enough, as though raising money can motivate a person through tough seasons—or that it could be worthwhile in and of itself. Granted, some people love fundraising; the whole process invigorates them. They love reaching a goal, completing a project, and checking all the boxes. However, when money is the ultimate goal, it can threaten everything else worth fighting for.

Years ago, a church connection introduced me to the Golden Girl Group Home in the little town of Ceredo, West Virginia. The cousin of our pastor's wife serves as the executive director of the home, and one day she invited me for a visit. She knew I worked in fundraising—and she knew my background—so, she thought I might be interested in the work she was doing.

Of course, she was right. Golden Girl serves teenage girls who have been abused, neglected, or orphaned. Growing up, I was a girl who was abused and neglected, and while I wasn't orphaned, I might as well have been; my parents' home was an unsafe place. I was very much on my own. I felt an immediate connection with the girls I met on my visit. My heart ached for them in a way it simply didn't for the boys at the Children's Center of Ohio (not that I didn't love them too). I also discovered that Golden Girl was in danger of closing its doors. It needed serious fundraising help. Even though I had a good job and liked what I did, I left it to start something new at Golden Girl. I never looked back, and I still love what I do to this day. I know I'm making a real difference every day.

As you can imagine, working with teenage girls can be difficult at times. And working with traumatized teenage girls can be downright messy. Sometimes, despite our best intentions, things don't go the way we hope. One time, several years after I began running the development office at Golden Girl, I became friends with a woman in the community I'll call Sharon.[1] She was someone I knew from church, but we also had connected in other circles. Sharon owned a local salon and had done quite well for herself. She was kind and generous, and she took an immediate interest in my work at Golden Girl.

Before long, Sharon became a faithful donor. But she did much more than give money; she advocated for our cause. Every year, she'd put together a fundraising event to benefit the home. It was wonderful. I'm certain her investment in the girls changed many lives. No doubt her generosity with time and money did a lot of good.

And then, one day, she did something simply amazing: She called and said she wanted to take one of the girls into her home to live with her. You see, all of the girls at Golden Girl are part of the state foster care system. That means a girl can eventually be placed in a foster home if the right situation opens up. Sharon loved the girls, and there was one particular sixteen-year-old girl who had a special place in her heart—we'll call her Mary. Sharon invited Mary to live with her.

While our campus is a wonderful place, and the girls form a tight community—some might even call it a family—we rejoice when one of our girls is placed in a healthy foster home. There's no substitute for a dedicated parent or two, and personalized attention can't be beat. I was excited for Sharon and Mary! At that point, Sharon was single, and, of course, Mary was without her family; they were creating their own little family together.

At first, that's exactly what happened. I remember hearing how Mary had started calling Sharon by the name Mom. For her part, Sharon treated Mary like her own daughter. She cared for her, provided for her, and made sure she felt completely secure in her new surroundings. The two of them got along fabulously, and they spent lots of time together. It was very sweet. From the outside, it looked like the kind of home life we wanted for all the girls.

Sometime later, however, the mood at Sharon's house changed. Because Sharon and I were friends, she began to confide in me. It started with little things —how she didn't understand Mary and there was too much teenage drama. Then she said the problem was really with her—she needed a break. Perhaps she bit off more than she could chew, and she needed a respite. I could understand that. I have kids, and I know what it's like to live with a teenager. There are times when it's hard to relate to them. There are times when you feel like you're at the end of your rope. That's all perfectly normal, and I imagine those feelings are heightened when the teenager comes with all the baggage of a troubled background. But I wasn't prepared for what Sharon told me next—she wanted to return Mary!

Sharon was talking about returning Mary to the foster care system the way one returns a pair of pants to the store. It sickened me. To understand what a big deal this is, you have to understand that returning Mary didn't mean sending her back to Golden Girl. That door was closed. Since Golden Girl works with the state to provide a stable environment for troubled girls, we don't have open beds. As soon as one girl leaves the program, their spot is taken by another girl in need. Even though Mary had been a part of our home before living with Sharon, she could not return when Sharon changed her mind. Instead, Mary would be put back into the foster system for a new placement. Who knew where she would have ended up?

Under no circumstances could I sit by and watch Sharon throw Mary's life into turmoil. I didn't know what had shifted in Sharon, but my focus at that point was on Mary. I needed to make sure she'd be okay. I'd take care of her myself if that's what it took. At that moment, there was a lot I wanted to say to Sharon about how she was behaving, but I held my tongue. I simply told her, "Mary can stay with me if you've decided she's too much for you right now."

But Sharon wasn't having it. She didn't want me to take Mary off her hands. She knew how that would look in our small community. People would be able to see the problem wasn't with Mary but with Sharon. She would look small, selfish, and cruel. Sharon wanted to keep up appearances—not do what was best for Mary—so she told me no. She had made up her mind to return Mary to the foster system and move on with her life.

I was devastated for Mary, and I was disappointed in Sharon. She had been and continued to be, one of Golden Girl's biggest supporters and financial contributors, but she failed to grasp our mission. We exist to help girls like Mary, not add more pain and rejection to their lives. I later found out what had changed for Sharon. Despite what she told me, the problem wasn't with Mary. Sharon had begun dating someone, and things became serious. All of a sudden, Mary was in the way. Sharon decided she didn't want the responsibility of raising a teenager. She wanted the freedom she had before she opened up her home. Caring only about herself, she decided Mary was no longer welcome in her house.

Very quickly I realized that advocating for Mary would mean opposing Sharon, very likely in a public setting. I would be violating one of the cardinal rules of fundraising—don't make your donors angry. I knew I would be choosing the welfare of Mary over my development goals for the home. It would cost me something significant to stand up for what was right.

At the time, I was working on the biggest project I'd ever undertaken (more on that in chapter 8), and I had a very important appointment related to the project. But I discovered Sharon had packed all of Mary's belongings into the car and planned to leave Mary at the courthouse. I arranged for a friend to attend the meeting in my place. I put the rest of my work on hold and went to the Boone County Courthouse to intervene. Though it felt like I was standing up to the system all on my own, I had a small group of friends by my side. They knew the situation and wanted to help. One of them was a Golden Girl donor who was licensed to be a foster parent in the state of West Virginia, and she was ready to take Mary home with her.

When I arrived, I didn't know what time the hearing was, and I didn't have legal cause to be there. I just knew I had to do something. When I got to the desk, I signed myself in. The woman behind the plexiglass asked me if I was with the case. I smiled and said, "Yes, I am." And that was enough to get into the courtroom. I suppose she thought I was an attorney, and I didn't say anything to change her perception. I found Mary's case worker and explained the situation. I told her I had someone who was licensed and willing to take Mary home with her that day—a friend from church. She told me Mary would need to go before the judge and tell him she had someone there to represent her, to help her, and to take her in. Most likely, the judge would grant her permission to stay in the new foster home.

Mary's social worker told me that if I hadn't come up with a solution, Sharon would have given Mary back to the system, with no place for Mary to go, and she would have had to sleep on the floor of the social worker's office at the courthouse overnight. Hearing that, I was so upset. I couldn't believe Sharon had it in her to be so cruel. But there it was. She didn't care about anyone but herself, and she was willing to see Mary suffer the trauma of being abandoned just to make her own life more comfortable. I would tell you that I was disgusted, but *disgusted* is too gentle a word for what I was feeling at that moment.

Thankfully, Mary's story has a happy ending. The judge granted our motion, and Mary went to stay with my licensed friend from church and eventually found a permanent home with a Golden Girl donor. She spent her remaining high school years being nurtured and supported by a wonderful, loving family. Today, Mary is married and has a beautiful baby girl. I was at her wedding, and as you can imagine, I was beaming from ear to ear.

I share this story with you because I know it's all too easy in discussions about fundraising strategies and development goals to keep first things first. But know this—fundraising is never the goal. Fundraising is always—always, always, always—a means to an end. The true goal of every development professional must be the good their organization is doing in the world. Raising money is a way to get there; it's the road, not the destination. There may come a time when you have to choose between pleasing a donor and upholding the mission of your organization. Don't fool yourself into believing the ends justify the means. They don't, not if you're compromising what's most important.

Your organization is not Golden Girl. You have your own mission, your own community, and your own priorities. But there are lots of Sharons out there in the world. Just remember: for every Sharon, there's also a Mary.

Always choose Mary.

Every. Single. Time.

She's counting on you.

CHAPTER THREE

HOW YOUR NONPROFIT IS LIKE A GREAT RESTAURANT

I met my husband Bobby when he was twenty-three and I was twenty-one. Though, admittedly, my life had taken a few more detours than his at that point, we were both trying to pay the bills by working at a restaurant as waitstaff. And while I always took pride in my work and did my best to provide great service to our guests, Bobby took great service to another level.

One time, Bobby had a table of two—a pair of sisters, senior citizens on a budget who had come to the restaurant to share an entrée. The item they ordered was a menu special, and it wasn't supposed to be shared. But Bobby always put his customers first. When the kitchen was done cooking the meal, he grabbed a second plate and painstakingly divided everything to feed two. It was extra work, and allowing two people to split a single entrée affected the check total—and thus, his potential tip—but none of that mattered to Bobby. He wanted to make sure every person who came into the restaurant felt seen and welcome.

Years later, after we were married and Bobby had achieved his dream of owning a restaurant, I watched that spark of hospitality light up his countenance nightly as familiar faces and new customers came in to eat. He loved to show people around, tell them about the food, and help them feel at home. And the thing is, he did it to a fault. One time, a guest wanted a dish that wasn't on the menu. But rather than deny them, Bobby ran out to a local grocery store, purchased the ingredients, and headed into the kitchen to make just what they wanted.

Right about now, you might be flipping back to check the cover of this book to make sure you're still reading about fundraising. I promise—this rabbit trail into the restaurant business has a purpose. You see, after years of running successful capital campaigns, I've discovered that great fundraising is a lot like a great restaurant.

We all know what it's like to eat at a restaurant that doesn't have good service. The food might be delicious, and the ambiance might be captivating, but if there isn't a welcoming spirit emanating from the host and waitstaff, the whole experience can seem cold and transactional. You may leave the restaurant with a full belly, but you'll soon forget the meal. What draws people back to a great eatery is the feeling they leave with. Loyalty is won or lost in that heart space.

Somehow, instinctively, we know this to be true of a restaurant experience, and yet when it comes to something much more important—fundraising for a cause we're passionate about—we are prone to fall back into transactional thinking. We get bogged down in the numbers, looking at financial goals and ROI (return on investment). And yet, at its core, fundraising is about welcoming other people into our passion. It's an invitation, not a transaction.

As I mentioned, my husband, Bobby, had a wonderful restaurant. His zeal for the business was so powerful that at one point he had restaurants in several locations. But after many years, competition grew stronger, and he decided to close up shop and move on to other endeavors. It was during that transition time that I began looking for work. Soon, I found a classified ad for a job at a children's home for delinquent youth called The Children's Center of Patriot, Ohio. The opening was for a childcare worker. I remember it paid something like eight dollars an hour. But the pay didn't matter to me. I loved at-risk kids because I had been one of them. So, I applied.

I met with the executive director, and he interviewed me for the position. Things went well, and a short time later he called to offer me the job—well, not exactly. From my résumé, he saw that I had launched YouthFest years earlier. He understood how much energy an event like that takes. He knew how much money it cost to keep it going year after year. He also knew that getting volunteers and donors to come together to cover all the needs and expenses doesn't happen without someone casting a vision and inviting all those people to work together for the common good. So, he offered me a job but not as a childcare worker; he wanted me to be the development director for the home.

I'll admit that when I was first starting, I had no idea what I was doing. I had done some pavement pounding to get YouthFest off the ground, and I had to raise money to break even every year, but that was an event, not an ongoing facility and program to help troubled teens. Though the home itself was in the middle of Amish country, most of the kids at the home were from the inner city. Many were former gang members. For some, this was the last stop before the juvenile hall, which is like a prison for those not old enough to serve time in a traditional correctional facility. Immediately, I felt a great weight on my shoulders, but perhaps that only strengthened my resolve. The kids were counting on me, and I wasn't going to let them down.

When I began my work at the Center, there was no previous development program, no list of donors, nothing. I had to start from scratch. Maybe it was a bit of my husband's hosting posture rubbing off on me, but my natural inclination was to create my own list and begin calling people and telling them about my cause. I invited my new connections to come to the home for a tour. I also networked—joining every community group I could. It was in those settings that I met more potential donors. I gave them tours too and answered their questions. I told them our success stories, and I listened. I let the donors tell me what projects and programs they were excited about.

Over the years, I've seen lots of development professionals lead with their lists. They have a series of funding goals, and when they interact with a donor, they tell the donor what they'd like money for. That's asking for a transaction, not extending an invitation. That's being a salesperson, not a host. On one level, I understand that way of thinking. There are real needs that have to be met, and no one wants to waste another person's time—they think it's best to get to the point.

But let's go back to the restaurant for a minute. Imagine being famished and sitting down to dinner, anticipating all the options you might savor. But instead of the server handing you a menu and letting you know about all the specials the chef has been preparing, she simply tells you what meal you'll be having for dinner. When you ask if there are other entrees to consider, she assures you this is the right entree for you. You might stay and try her sole recommendation, or you might leave and find another restaurant more accommodating to your tastes and preferences. But whatever you decide that particular evening, you will not feel seen or appreciated, and you probably won't return.

Do you see what I'm getting at? People who give to charities and nonprofits typically enjoy doing so. It's a treat for them just as much as it is a treat for the organizations they support. Help them find joy in it! **Welcome donors (and potential donors) to see and experience what you're excited about.** Listen to their ideas and their passions. Donors want to feel special, not necessarily for the sake of their pride but because they want to know you see them, not just the checks you hope they'll write. And that means every interaction is important.

Several years ago, I received an email from someone who wasn't connected to our nonprofit. It wasn't a past donor, just someone who said they might be interested in supporting the work we were doing, but first, they needed to see an annual report. Now, a lot of people don't respond to emails like that right away, viewing them as more of a nuisance than the real work of development. However, if you recognize that the role of a fundraising professional is to invite people into the vital work of the nonprofit that you're representing, there is no such thing as an unimportant person.

I responded immediately, and I pointed them to our website where our annual report was hosted and available for download. I thought that would be the end of it, but I received a reply to my email. Apparently, the link I sent was broken, and the annual report was woefully out of date. Rather than falling into the trap that such things are "someone else's problem"—I wasn't responsible for updating the website or getting our annual report out on time—I talked to our CFO, got the current annual report, and responded to the inquirer as quickly as I could. (Again, just like a high-quality restaurant, it's important to respond to the needs of your donors—your guests—quickly!)

A week after that email exchange, I received an envelope in the mail. Tucked inside was a check for $50,000. I think it's safe to say that a generous donor would have given that gift to another organization if I had neglected the email or moved on to "more important things" after discovering the annual report was out of date. Every donor, and every potential donor, is important. So make sure you treat them accordingly—you never know what effect your care might have!

As I mentioned in the previous chapter, after leaving The Children's Center, I began working for the Golden Girl Group Home in Ceredo, West Virginia—a place with a mission that's dear to my heart. Of course, my passion for the work of Golden Girl has me talking to everyone who will listen.

By networking, I've met wonderful people who have come alongside us to help these at-risk girls get their young lives back on track. And because I've invited these friends into the work we're doing, they've caught a bit of my passion, and they pass it on to others. **Just as word of mouth creates a powerful buzz for a restaurant, it can do the same for a nonprofit.**

Networking is powerful because, if done right, everyone helps everyone else. For me, that often means referrals. One time, while I was on vacation at the beach with my family, I received a phone call from a business owner I'd met through a networking group. She told me she met a landscaper who wanted to donate his services to the home. She said I needed to call him right away. I tried to explain that I was on vacation and would call him the following week, but she insisted I call him sooner than later. So, from the beach, I gave the potential donor a call. And I'm glad I did.

I arranged a time for him to visit Golden Girl. He wanted to be there when the girls got off the bus from school. He wanted to see the work we were doing first-hand and check out our facilities. After I returned from my trip, I gave him a tour, and he liked what he saw. Then he told me he wanted to help. I thought, being a landscaper, he might want to donate a tree or something. Little did I know I was about to undertake a significant renovation project. It was going to cost somewhere in the neighborhood of $250,000 to build a new community building, renovate a courtyard, and create a new outdoor seating area that could be used for counseling sessions.

As it turned out, he was not only a landscaper; he was the president of the Tri-State Landscaping Association. Every three years, this association, which included his business and those of all his competitors, donated to a worthy nonprofit. He told me that he had chosen mine. He donated funding, materials, and labor for the entire project—the building and the outdoor renovations. Up to that point, it was the single largest project I'd undertaken, and that one connection helped make it a reality. Boy, I am glad I called!

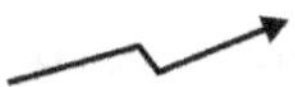

Do you remember how I told you about the time my husband, Bobby, went to the market to buy ingredients for a dish he didn't offer on the menu because a customer wanted it? I know—it seems a bit extreme. But think about it for a minute. That diner will never forget it. I'm sure he felt special. He probably told all of his friends about what Bobby did for him. And I'm sure he returned to eat at the restaurant again and again.

I understand that in the restaurant world, it's not always possible to have a "whatever you want" policy. After all, there's a reason we have menus. Cooks can't be learning new recipes all day and night. Something similar is true in the nonprofit world. An organization can't (and shouldn't) shift its mission to meet a donor's desires, no matter how much support is on the table. However, every development professional must try to foster the same attitude my husband displayed the night he made that special meal. **Giving donors what they need is one way of inviting them into the good work taking place.** Let me explain what I mean.

Years ago, two women wanted to set up a dance clinic for some of the girls at the home. However, dance classes were not on my list of new programs to create. What I needed was funding for a building project. I could have politely declined their offer and moved on to other endeavors that promised to produce more funding. But I never want to turn anyone away who wants to help, so I agreed to let them come. I even talked to several of the girls about the opportunity and helped them get excited about it.

The day came, and it was a lot of fun. The girls who participated loved it, and I could tell our two visitors enjoyed sharing their gifts and passion. As we were chatting afterward, I discovered one of the women was an executive at a large equipment manufacturer. I asked if they had a fund to donate to nonprofits. She said, "As a matter of fact, we do!" I asked if we could meet the following week to discuss it. She agreed, and that conversation led to another and then another. A short time later, I was looking at a check for $20,000!

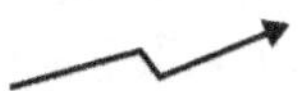

Another time, I received a call from Amanda at Toyota Manufacturing of Buffalo, West Virginia. I'd met Amanda before, as she had helped the girl's home with a small grant from the company. She asked if she and a few others from the Toyota plant could volunteer to do some work around the property. I told her we'd love that, and we set up an appointment for me to show her around.

Amanda shared that a lot of the nonprofits she had called didn't return her phone calls. The ones she did get in touch with said they were only interested in monetary donations; they weren't looking for volunteers. Sadly, it seemed those organizations weren't interested in meeting their donors' needs, only in meeting financial goals. I learned that sometimes letting the donor decide what's on the menu works out better than I could ever plan. That instance, with the kind folks at Toyota, turned out to be no exception.

I showed Amanda around the property, and she saw that one of our houses was dilapidated. She decided that's where she and her team would begin. Before long, she pulled me aside and said it felt like she was just putting lipstick on a pig. The building needed more than cosmetic repairs; it needed a major overhaul, and that would require more people and more materials.

Oh, I should probably tell you that this all happened shortly after the 2011 earthquake in the Pacific Ocean that caused a forty-foot tsunami to pound the island of Japan. Because of that disaster, Toyota's headquarters was out of commission and parts and materials were not being sent to the plant in Buffalo, which meant the employees could not do their jobs. Toyota's corporate culture is such that layoffs and furloughs are avoided at all costs. Toyota of Buffalo was looking for work to give to their employees, and many of them came to Golden Girl.

The plant operated nearly around the clock, so workers showed up at all hours of the day and night to fill their shifts. My job was to get them what they needed. I made more trips to Home Depot than I could count. In a relatively short time, they had gutted, renovated, and upgraded a house that desperately needed it. Toyota even got some of its manufacturing partners involved. (Nitro Electric from nearby Nitro, West Virginia, installed a new electrical system throughout the building.)

Here's the amazing thing about all of this: That house needed repairs and a refresh—anyone walking by could have seen it—but we would never have had the funding or the manpower to do a complete renovation. I never would have asked. But because I let the donors tell me what they wanted to do for us, we received a blessing we weren't looking for!

Before I leave this restaurant analogy, I want to give you one more piece of advice. **Show your donors the beautiful, tantalizing steak, but don't talk about how the cow was butchered.** One of the biggest mistakes development professionals make is giving people more information than they need. Most donors don't want to know the ins and outs of your organization. They don't want to know the darkest bits of case files. They don't want to hear about every challenge your organization is facing. They do, however, want to hear about your successes. They want to know how their donations make a real difference in the lives of real people. And, above all, they want to know that your organization is making the world a better place.

Like a great restauranteur, you have a lot to offer potential donors. And if you're doing your job well, you have a lot to be proud of and a lot to show off. Invite people in, get to know what they want, and serve them up something special!

When I first began working at Golden Girl, the needs were overwhelming. Most of the buildings needed significant renovations, the campus needed additional facilities and a major refresh, and something in our programming needed to change so older girls who were stepping out on their own wouldn't fall through the cracks. And then, of course, there was the home's annual operating budget, which had to be met or there wouldn't be a home for much longer.

That annual budget is unrelenting. It's always there, needing more money, more attention, more time. I know, it can be hard to think about special projects when your organization is trying to tread water and stay afloat. But here's what I've learned: Rarely will a new donor give to the general fund. What brings them in are new projects.

It's human nature. People want to be part of something exciting and groundbreaking. They want to meet a real-world need, not maintain the status quo. But once these same people bring a project to life, they're much more likely to partner with your nonprofit for the long haul. They become invested in the organization, in the community, and in the lives of the people you're serving. All that to say, it's essential that you think about projects not as intrusive add-ons but as a necessary part of your fundraising strategy.

Many years ago, when my grandmother came to the United States from Poland, she was a single mother of five. My grandfather had been killed in a tragic accident, so my grandmother was left to care for her children by herself. To make matters worse, it was during the Great Depression. She was poor—and I mean bare-cupboards poor—and she was about to give up.

My grandmother looked at the faces of her five children. They were hungry, and she didn't have anything to feed them. At that moment, she could no longer hold herself together. She began to weep in front of her kids—something she had tried not to do because she wanted them to believe everything was going to be alright. But suddenly, she wasn't so sure.

That's when my Aunt Stella, who was just a young girl at the time, said something that changed the whole situation. She reminded my grandmother that they did have a few things to eat. There were carrots, and there was a bit of milk that hadn't turned yet. And there were spices. "We could make carrot soup," she suggested.

My grandmother wiped the tears from her eyes and mustered a smile. She told Stella, "Yes. Yes, we can," and she got to work. She peeled the carrots, chopped them, and dropped the pieces in a pot of milk on the stove. In a few minutes, she was serving her five children homemade carrot soup. From what I've been told, it turned out delicious, simple but elegant, and flavorful—the sort of soup that might be served before the main course at a gourmet restaurant these days.

My grandmother thought she had nothing to feed her kids that day, but as it turned out, she had all the ingredients right there in her kitchen. She just needed to be reminded of what she had, and she needed to envision what they could become. I think about that story often as I'm working on projects for the girls' home. Back when I was just starting in fundraising, I learned that some of the best projects come from ingredients we already have.

Before I began my role as development director, the home had nothing in the way of fundraising initiatives, except one small program—Christmas Angel. At the holidays, donors could sponsor a girl by giving money or purchasing items on her Christmas list. The goal was to raise $200 for each girl. My predecessor had a small rolodex of donors who gave to the program each year. There was nothing wrong with the effort—each year, the girls received Christmas gifts—but it wasn't moving anything in terms of donor engagement. When I took over, I decided to enlarge Christmas Angel, and it became an entry point into our organization.

I invited donors, new and old, to get involved by shopping for presents from the girls' lists. I told them about the girls they were shopping for and about our organization. I discovered that most of the men and women with whom I engaged wanted to do more than simply give money during the holidays. They wanted to buy special gifts for the girls beyond what we were asking for. They also wanted to bring surprises, decorate the houses on campus, and throw Christmas parties. Of course, none of those individual acts of kindness was a gamechanger for Golden Girl, but collectively, over a few weeks, they changed the tone of our donor relationships. And all I did was take ingredients we already had to make something new.

If you think about it, that's all a good recipe is, isn't it? It's taking foods you have and combining them to make something new. That's what I did with one of our programs for our older girls. You see, when the residents of Golden Girl turn eighteen, they transition into an independent living situation. That doesn't mean they're out of the program, but it does mean they do more on their own. To help them as they step into a new phase, we have life coaches come alongside them and offer guidance.

This life coach program existed long before I came on board, but I could see it needed a significant lift. I treated it as a program in need of funding—which it was—and I crafted a narrative about the importance of life coaches and the good they do for our girls. I highlighted several success stories and cast a vision for the future. We weren't planning on changing much, just doing more with what we already had. However, presenting the program to donors as an opportunity to change lives proved to be powerful. I tell you this because sometimes the best "new" program isn't new at all. Any existing program can be brought into the spotlight and used as a doorway to invite donors in.

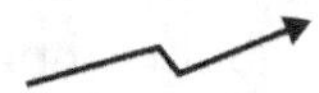

Launching a new program can be a time-consuming, energy-zapping endeavor. In most cases, there's research required to determine the precise needs to be met. And while you're doing that, you might as well research potential sources of funding to be tapped. There are events to plan, phone calls to make, meetings to arrange, and people to meet. And some unforeseen obstacles and roadblocks must be overcome along the way. If it were possible to see across weeks and months (and sometimes years), it would be enough to bring even the best development professionals to their knees, overwhelmed and exhausted before ever starting.

With that in mind, what I'm going to suggest next might sound a little crazy at first. I have found that my most successful seasons are those when I have multiple projects in motion. At any given time, some are nearing completion, others are just getting started, and others are somewhere in between.

There are a few reasons I like to have several projects going at once. First, moving ahead on lots of projects at the same time means no one project can stall all the others. For example, if a renovation gets delayed, I can keep pressing on with our mentorship program or our Christmas fundraiser. I can shift gears easily without losing momentum.

Second, I learn a lot as I go. What applies to one project might very well help with another. All this real-world learning has helped me develop a sixth sense. At times, I'm able to solve potential problems before they even surface, simply because another project has trained me well.

Finally, and most importantly, multiple projects allow me to serve our donors more efficiently. When I speak to an existing donor or meet a potential one, I have lots to talk about. What I've found is that, as I'm talking about my projects, there's usually one or two that will speak to a donor's heart. If I have quite a few to discuss, the more likely something will pique their interest. One person might love building projects, while another finds those daunting and would be more interested in helping with a fundraising event. One might have a special connection to a landscaping business and would be willing to help renovate our campus, while another might want to fund an enrichment program for the girls. I believe fundraising should be donor-centric, so I always have something for any and every donor who wants to partner with us.

One word of warning for when you're juggling several projects at once: Don't get ahead of yourself. I made that mistake one time. Early on in my tenure with Golden Girl, I was faced with a big task. One of the dormitory houses was in terrible shape. I don't just mean it needed a facelift; I mean it was infested with rodents! No matter what we did, we couldn't seem to stop the mice from getting in.

As you can imagine, it was a terrible living situation for the girls. We knew something had to be done, and we tried everything. But I eventually resolved to build an entirely new house. I connected with the West Virginia Housing Development Fund and explained what I wanted to do and how much money we needed for the project. The man I worked with was enthusiastic about our mission and wanted to help, and he gave me a verbal agreement for a significant amount of the funding.

I was thrilled, and I began to make plans. I was so eager to begin! I got the girls moved out and into temporary housing, and I had the mouse-infested building demolished so we could begin prepping the site for a brand-new house. The only problem was, when I called the West Virginia Housing Development Fund to let them know I was ready to proceed with the promised grant, I discovered the man I had been working with—the one who had given me the verbal go-ahead the last time we spoke—was no longer employed there; he had moved out of state. No one else at the Housing Development Fund knew a thing about my project, and they could not guarantee funding.

I was devastated, embarrassed, and terrified. *What if they say no? What if we can't rebuild? What if I can't figure out a way to correct this mistake?* Those were the thoughts swirling around in my head as I scrambled to fill out all of the necessary paperwork needed to reapply for the grant. Thankfully, in the end, it all worked out. The Housing Development Fund did indeed see the value in the work we do, and they supplied the necessary funding to complete the project. I was no worse for the wear, but I learned two valuable lessons. The first is to get financial commitments in writing before moving forward, and the second is to pick myself up, dust off my knees, and try again when things seem to be falling apart. That's good advice for fundraising and all of life!

The house we built had ten rooms in it. Instead of soliciting funds for furniture and décor, I invited donors to sponsor a room. They could give financially or go shopping with me for beds and dressers and lamps and such. The result was that many of our kind donors got to know the girls who would be living in "their room," and they outfitted the new living space according to the girls' tastes. Many of the rooms were tied together with a theme. Even though I made a colossal mistake by tearing down the house before I had secured the necessary funding to rebuild, the whole thing turned out better than I could have anticipated. Not only did the donors feel a new and deeper connection with Golden Girl, but each of the rooms turned out very special, much better than we could have done if we simply bought the same functional pieces for every room.

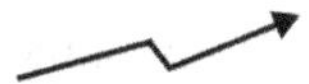

Something else I've learned about fundraising over the years is that my campaigns are much more successful when I remember fundraising isn't really about raising money; it's about telling a compelling story. Don't misunderstand. I'm not suggesting you should take your eye off the bottom line. The receipts are how you'll measure your success because every dollar translates into the good work your nonprofit is all about. However, simply asking people for money usually won't get the job done. Instead, you need to tell them a captivating story—and projects are one way to make those stories come to life.

For example, while many people in our community know Golden Girl helps at-risk teenage girls, most don't know that our work continues even after the girls turn eighteen. We provide career training, college prep, mentoring, and other help as they learn to navigate adult life. And as I mentioned earlier, as the young women age out of the on-campus program, they transition to independent housing.

Initially, the independent housing we had to offer the girls was spread across the city—an apartment here, another one there, you get the idea. The problem was that it was a bit too independent for many of the girls in our program. Overnight, the community they had enjoyed on campus was gone. The security they knew was somewhat diminished too. They were left feeling vulnerable. What made things worse is that oftentimes a girl's family would invite her to come home, in many cases providing a haven for their abuser to return. The insecurity of a new living situation would make such offers attractive. Having been homeless myself, I didn't want to see a girl graduate from our residential program and face the uncertainty that comes with a compromised living situation. I didn't want to see a young girl, especially someone who already had a rough start in life, make a decision based on fear. I decided something had to be done. I knew we could do better.

I had it in my mind to build a beautiful, new apartment complex to house girls eighteen and older. It would be a truly transitional place. The girls would be off campus and yet not out on their own. With that vision in my heart, I got to work.

The first thing I needed was a location. Early on, a donor offered me a parcel of land near the railroad tracks. I was elated! I also found out that I could receive funding by accessing money available through our local bank. I didn't know that until I began asking questions, but the federal government requires banks to invest in their local communities. It's called the Community Reinvestment Act. Every bank has a fund to assist with low-income housing and projects that help the poor.

Our apartment complex qualified, so I applied and was approved. The only stipulation was that we needed to have a project that was ready to go. I thought we were ready, given that I had a piece of land to build on. But when we conducted an environmental assessment of the plot, which is required by law, I found out there was a problem well below the surface —gas tanks buried deep within the soil. As it was, we would not be able to build on our land without remedying the environmental danger.

Suddenly, I found myself with money to build but no place to do it. Worse than that, my CRA-granted funding had a deadline. If I couldn't find a new piece of real estate suitable for an apartment complex soon, I'd lose that investment. I wanted to panic, but I knew I couldn't. I didn't have time for that! So, I did what comes most naturally—I continued networking. One of my contacts told me there was a beautiful property five minutes from our main campus, and they believed the owner might be willing to donate it.

The property was everything I was told, so I called the owner and asked him to come down and check out Golden Girl. I wanted to give him a tour of our facilities and tell him about our programs. At first, I couldn't get him to meet with me. As it turned out, he was something of a character—a very wealthy businessman and kind of eccentric. At one point, he was supposed to be a contestant on the television series *The Apprentice*. He was boisterous, and his personality could be overwhelming for some people. But that didn't deter me. I kept asking, kept pursuing, and kept following up with him. Eventually, he gave in. I don't want to say I wore him down because I wasn't rude or anything; I just didn't give up.

He came to the home and met with me. I showed him around, explained what I wanted to do for the older girls, and asked him if he would consider donating his property to our cause. To my relief, he told me he loved what we were doing for the community and said he would be more than happy to donate the land. I was relieved, to say the least!

The land and the CRA funding were just the beginning of the battle. I still had to raise the rest of the money for construction, not to mention furnishings and landscaping. Because there was so much to do, I got lots of people involved. The local hospital agreed to furnish the community room. To save money, I had students from a nearby vocational school do the electrical work—that is until the state threatened to fine us $3,000 per student! At that point, I found a licensed electrician who convinced a couple of friends to help him with the remainder of the work and graciously agreed to donate his time. Our general contractor understood what we were trying to do, and he helped me connect with local businesses willing to donate materials and labor. Seeing all those people in our community come together to help was a beautiful thing.

In the end, the apartment complex turned out better than I hoped. Those eleven apartments—five two-bedroom and six one-bedroom units—not only changed the nature of our program for young women, it also changed lives. When it was done, something inside of me changed too. I felt like I could take on any challenge. No project was too big, and no dollar amount was too high. If my girls needed it, I would find a way. That's why, when the mayor of our small town of Ceredo, West Virginia, approached me with a proposal that could, once again, change our program at the home for the better, I jumped at the opportunity.

I'm used to approaching city officials to ask for donations, grants, and help with a project now and then, but it was unusual when the mayor approached me. Needless to say, I was intrigued. It turned out the mayor knew of three adjacent properties near downtown that he wanted Golden Girl to make use of. He loved our program and wanted to see the lots put to good use.

As things stood, one had a dilapidated house, another a vacant house owned by the bank, and the final one had an abandoned building. The thing was, the city didn't own any of the land; it would be up to me to purchase it. The mayor told me that if I could secure the deeds, the city would donate the excavation and clear the three lots at no charge. After that, it would be up to us to build something worthy of the girls we served.

At Golden Girl, we want to do more than provide a safe environment for our girls; we also want to set them on the right path for life. That's why we provide educational opportunities, life mentoring, and career training. However, I knew we could do so much more if only we had the property facilities. The three connected lots would provide enough room to create something truly special.

I was all in.

When I got to work, I discovered it wouldn't be a simple matter of raising the money and buying the three properties. Instead, each one had its own set of issues. Two of the buildings had liens on the property, which would need to be lifted before any sale could take place. The other—the residential property—had a family living there. I'd need to find another place for them to live before I could purchase the lot. Over the next few months, I kicked my fundraising efforts into high gear, looked for a suitable new home for a soon-to-be-displaced family, and researched what it would take to get the liens removed from the adjacent properties.

Although it was a unique situation, I have found that most large projects are like that to some extent.

Each new day is an opportunity to chip away at obstacles by raising money, learning new things, networking, and investigating the unknown. These efforts often require the skills of an amateur sleuth, the ability to find all the clues to figure out solutions. When the project is over, however, you can look back and know it was all worth it.

In this case, I was able to clear up the financial and legal issues that hampered the three properties, have the old buildings bulldozed to the ground and hauled away, and break ground on a brand-new, first-of-its-kind building in our little town. The Golden Minds Center for Learning and Development has become such a special part of Golden Girl that it's hard to imagine our program without it. On the first floor, there's Golden Treasures—a boutique and consignment shop operated by the girls. People can donate clothes and household items. Some of what is given goes to the girls, but everything else is sold in the store. And of course, all the profits go back into the programs at Golden Girl. Above that space, on the second floor, there's a state-of-the-art classroom, where the girls learn from professionals across a variety of fields. Next to that is our tea room, where we host get-togethers and celebrate special occasions as a community.

The Golden Minds Center has become a wonderful extension of everything we're doing on the main campus of Golden Girl. Our residents are learning real-life skills and being exposed to the wisdom and encouragement of professionals from throughout the community. As they learn and grow, they're contributing to the very programs that support them. In addition, as we've stepped out into the community, we've attracted new supporters and word of mouth about the good work we're doing has spread like never before. When I'm in the building and look around at all that takes place within those walls, it's difficult to remember the small battles I had to fight to make it a reality. But that's how big change usually happens—one small step at a time.

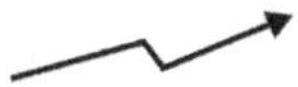

If I could sit down with you over a cup of coffee and offer a bit of advice about taking on projects, it would be this: Don't let the size of your project intimidate you. For every project, no matter how big, there is a path forward. Your job is to figure out, little by little, where that path lies. You don't have to have all the answers before you begin, and you don't have to do everything all at once. You will make mistakes—and that's okay. Mistakes are how we learn, and they are part of the process. In many cases, it's hard to know what to do until you've stumbled a few times into what not to do.

Celebrate your milestones, and don't give up. Above all, try to have fun. Every difficult project is a puzzle to solve, and it feels good when you find pieces that fit and the final picture starts to come into view. In the end, you'll have brought something into the world that wasn't there before—something that resonates with your passions and offers something good. And things like that are always worth it.

You may recall from chapter two that my first full-time job in development was at The Children's Center of Patriot, Ohio. I was offered the position based largely on my experience organizing and orchestrating YouthFest every year. As I stepped into the role, I knew a thing or two about what it takes to pull off a large concert event. My boss, R.W. Boggs, suspected as much. That's why, not too long after starting in that role, he approached me about a fundraising idea.

What unfolded over the next several months was one of the most educational experiences of my career. That's because I made nearly every mistake possible as I set about bringing R.W.'s vision to life. The event I put together was a failure—and nearly a financial disaster as well. But we'll get to all that…

R.W. knew I could get big-name stars to come to our sleepy little part of the country. I'd done it before with Grammy-winning recording artists for YouthFest. The only difference was that R.W. wasn't a fan of Christian music; he was into heavy metal and hard rock. In particular, he wanted me to bring Joan Jett and the Blackhearts to town.

In theory, there's nothing wrong with getting someone like Joan Jett to headline a fundraising concert. But something deep inside told me it was a bad idea, and I should have spoken up. That was my first mistake. As my good friend Alys Smith likes to say, "Women should have the power to say no and the courage to say yes." But that's not just true for women; it applies to all people. I should have gone with my gut and told R.W. I thought a Joan Jett concert was a bad idea.

A fundraising event needs to be a good fit for the organization, for the donors, and for the community. Joan Jett certainly has name recognition, but her music didn't sync with our mission to help troubled boys, nor was she someone who would necessarily appeal to many of our donors. On top of that, Gallipolis, Ohio, is a rural and very traditional area—not exactly Joan Jett country. But as I said, I didn't speak up.

Putting on a concert for charity is a huge undertaking, requiring lots of sponsors, volunteers, and planning. If that were all I'd needed to do, it would have been a challenge by itself. But R.W. wasn't done yet. There was more he wanted to pack into the event. You see, there was another local event in the area called Mega Bash. At Mega Bash, for a $100 raffle ticket, people got the chance to win cars, boats, motorcycles, and other valuable prizes. In all, there were more than $1 million worth of prizes. The possibility of winning a shiny, new vehicle brought lots of people to Mega Bash. Thinking it would draw the same large crowds, R.W. wanted to have the same type of raffle for the Joan Jett concert, and it was up to me to secure all the prizes and sell all the tickets.

Before I could book Joan Jett—or any other artist for that matter—I needed to find a venue. R.W. told me he wanted to use the fairgrounds in town. To accommodate thousands of attendees, we needed a large site, so I looked into it. I was able to reserve the space, but there was just one problem: We weren't allowed to serve alcohol on the premises. That wasn't a problem for me, but as I thought about who might want to see Joan Jett perform, I knew the lack of alcohol would be an issue. Also, with the big raffle we would be holding, there would surely be plenty of gamblers. They, too, would want to drink. Still, R.W. wasn't deterred. He wanted to push forward, with or without the freedom to serve beer.

I met with the owners of car dealerships, boat dealerships, and the Harley Davidson dealership in town to explain what I was trying to do. Many of them graciously agreed to set aside vehicles that I could purchase at cost for the raffle. I decided we'd sell two tiers of tickets. Most of the prizes would be part of the main raffle—the one people could be a part of for a $100 ticket. But we'd also have an early bird raffle. Those tickets would be $50 each, and the prize would be a brand-new Harley Davidson Screaming Eagle motorcycle.

With a raffle like that, you're supposed to sell enough raffle tickets to cover the cost of all the prizes. That way, you're not at risk of promising something you can't deliver. But as we began selling tickets, we quickly realized we were in trouble. We weren't selling nearly enough to cover all the cars, boats, and motorcycles we had planned to raffle off. We didn't even sell enough to cover the Screaming Eagle Harley Davidson! Though the event was fast approaching, we needed a Plan B.

Stressed out one night at home, I explained my dilemma to my husband, Bobby, and, as he often does, he had a brilliant idea. "Convert the $100 tickets into $50 ones," he suggested. He was right. If we made the raffle all about the Harley, we might be able to cover the cost. Maybe. We hadn't yet sold enough tickets to pay for the motorcycle, but there was still time. Achieving that goal was at least possible. And if we converted the tickets and still didn't sell enough of them, at least our loss would be more manageable.

Soon, I had everyone who works at The Children's Center on the phone talking to ticketholders, trying to convince them to convert their $100 tickets into two $50 early bird tickets. Some people were upset. Some even demanded their money back, but in the end, we made it work—at least as well as we could. And I learned a valuable lesson I will never forget. **When planning a fundraiser, make sure everything is paid for before the event itself.** Today, I don't hold events that aren't paid for ahead of time. I do this through sponsorships and ticket sales, but also by keeping things realistic. I would never again promise more than $1 million in prizes and hope for the best.

When the day of the concert and raffle came, it was clear to everyone that things hadn't gone according to plan. Joan Jett performed—and she put on a great show with a lot of energy—but there were only one hundred or so people in attendance. I felt terrible. Joan Jett and the Blackhearts were used to playing for huge crowds, and we hoped to have at least three thousand to four thousand people there. Needless to say, I was embarrassed.

Joan was a total professional about the whole thing.

She was more concerned about the boys' home than she was about the small crowd. I wanted to thank Joan for coming, so a few days before the concert, I bought her a small Bible with a black metal cover. I had read that her childhood had been nearly as rough as mine, so I could think of nothing more precious to share with the famous rocker than God's Word—plus, with the black metal, it looked like a Bible that would be at home with Joan Jett.

I wrote a note inside the front cover of the Bible, and I gave it to Joan just before she left the fairgrounds after the concert. Then I prayed with her and told her a bit of my story. As I did, I could see tears forming in her eyes. A few minutes later, Joan's manager approached me with a message from Joan. "Joan wants you to know that if you ever need anything, she'll be there for you." Being able to have that interaction with Joan Jett made the whole event worth it—even if it wasn't a financial success.

When it came to the raffle, we never did sell enough tickets to pay for the Harley Davidson Screaming Eagle. As the numbers were being pulled to reveal the lucky winning ticket, I looked on with knots in my stomach, wanting the whole thing to be over. Instead of raising money for the home, we were poised to lose quite a bit of money. The whole event seemed like such a financial waste.

When the number was called, a man came forward, but rather than smiling from ear to ear, he had an unsettled look on his face. He whispered something into R.W.'s ear and R.W. whispered back. Then something wonderful happened. The gentleman said he would rather *not* accept the motorcycle. I was dumbfounded! It was a free motorcycle—a very fancy one at that. But it was wonderful news! Later, R.W.

told me the man—a local doctor—had asked if he would need to pay taxes on the retail price of the Harley. When R.W. told him yes, the doctor decided he would rather donate the motorcycle back to The Children's Center.

I consider what happened with the Screaming Eagle to be a small miracle. When all was said and done, we still lost some money on the event—several thousand dollars at least—but the damage wasn't nearly as bad as it could have been. Looking back on that entire season, I realized I was constantly reacting to challenges and trying to make the best of a crumbling situation. I never want to be in that situation again, being reactive rather than proactive.

There are no guarantees in life. Even the most meticulously planned event can go sideways, and oftentimes it's due to circumstances that can't be controlled. That's why **you must have not only a Plan A for your event, but also a Plan B, a Plan C, and even a Plan D.** Make sure you know what you will do to achieve your goals for the event if things begin to fall apart. Your event may not turn out as you imagined, but you won't be caught off guard. And you'll have a story with fewer twists and turns than mine!

As you might suspect, after surviving the Joan Jett/Harley Davidson fiasco, I've developed some best practices for events. For starters, at Golden Girl, I hold only two major events each year. While I might participate in other smaller events in between—speaking or networking, I have chosen to focus my energy on two, and only two, events for the home. Any more than that, and I find it's hard to build excitement. **Donors are busy people, and if it appears there's always something going on, they're more likely to tune out.** So, I keep things simple.

When I first became the development director at Golden Girl, I inherited an event held each spring in connection with the Kentucky Derby. We rent space at the Guyan Country Club for a delicious mid-morning meal, and all the women come out wearing their big, beautiful Derby hats. It's called the Hats Off Derby Brunch, and it's a lot of fun. It's been happening for several years now, so it's become something of a local tradition not to be missed.

One of the reasons I love the event is that it can be big or small and still be successful. If we sell lots of tickets, I can expand our space and order more food. If we sell fewer tickets than anticipated, I can cut back on the menu. No matter what, I am in control and can make adjustments as needed. But here's the thing: I don't hold the Derby Brunch to raise money. My goal is to break even.

Before you begin planning an event, it's important to know what your objectives are. In our case, I don't believe the Derby Brunch has the potential to be a big fundraiser, but it's a great time that helps generate a lot of enthusiasm for our mission. Every year, I turn strangers and acquaintances into friends and donors. Since we break even each time, the brunch essentially costs us nothing. And for the low, low price of zero dollars, I have a captive audience of women who are willing to come out in support of Golden Girl. I get to share my heart and tell them about the important work taking place in our community.

But these women don't need much inspiration.

They're already so passionate about wanting to help the home that one year several of them came forward with an idea. They wanted to hold a silent auction at the brunch, but I wasn't sure it would work. I didn't know if the women who attended the brunch would want to go into another area of the restaurant to bid on items. I thought it might take away from the spirit of the day. But I decided to let the women have at it. As I said earlier, I love it when donors want to step in and take ownership. I figured we could always try the silent auction, and if it didn't work, we would just go back to the way things were before.

It started with a handmade quilt, but the wonderful donors went to different shops around town and got items donated to the cause. When the day finally came, I still wasn't sure it would work, but to my surprise, it was a big success. In total, the auction raised $7,000 for the home. My break-even event became a wonderful fundraiser that's now more fun than ever.

The other event I hold each year is a concert, but unlike R W. with the Joan Jett show, I chose an artist more likely to appeal to our donors and community at large. The Crabb Family is a Grammy award-winning southern gospel group. In our part of the country, faith runs deep, so gospel music resonates a bit more than hard rock. Also, many churches in the area are eager to contribute to the mission of Golden Girl. When the Crabb Family comes to town, it's not difficult to get churches to sponsor the event since they know the message emanating from the stage will be aligned with their own.

When I consider an entertainer, I try to check a

few boxes. First, are they likely to draw a crowd? A performer might be talented, but if they don't have much name recognition, it will be hard to build your audience. Second, do they have a substantial local following? If it's a musician, previous tour schedules will reveal if they have fans in the area. You also can ask around and get people's impressions. Just be careful you're talking to people who know they can be honest with you. Too often, people try to be polite by telling you what they think you want to hear. Finally, I check them out first. By catching their act, listening to their latest album, or watching a performance on television, you can get a sense of what your event might be like.

Booking an entertainer with a following is essentially borrowing their platform for your organization, so make sure it's one you want to borrow. In the case of the Crabb Family, they check all the boxes. That's why we've had them come to our small corner of the world ten years in a row.

One of the secrets to a successful event is to **know who your potential sponsors are and create an event likely to appeal to them.** As I mentioned, many of our sponsors are churches, so the Crabb Family fits right in. Of course, by saying your event should be aligned with your sponsors, I don't mean you shouldn't consider other donors or your community. But if your sponsors feel a connection to the event, it will be easier to stay on top of your budget. Remember: if you can cover costs before the event begins, you ensure success.

Speaking of sponsors, **when you introduce your event to a potential sponsor, it's important to be clear about what you're offering.** In other words, tell them precisely what they will receive for their donation. I usually put together a printed information packet with our logo on it that outlines the different levels of sponsorship and the prices. It lets business owners know that their gift is tax deductible and describes all the options available. These might include their logo on banners, a live mention from the stage, their organization's inclusion in the program, or other bits of publicity. However, rather than making things à la carte, I create tiers with standard price points to keep things simple.

One last essential for events: No matter what your goal is for an event—whether it's networking, exposure, or fundraising—**be sure you have a way to capture names, email addresses, and any other contact information you deem important.** That way you can build your pool of potential donors and rabid fans while keeping them abreast of all that's going on with your nonprofit.

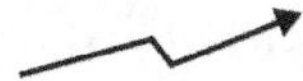

If done right, events will help sustain and grow your mission. But they can also be a lot of fun. There's something beautiful about seeing people who love and care about your cause gather together in support of it. Enjoy the process, learn as you go, and remember what you're working for. It's always worth it in the end —even when the event doesn't go exactly as planned.

When I agreed to become the development director at the Golden Girl Group Home, I had a few conditions. First, I told the executive director I couldn't be micromanaged. I needed the freedom to do the job how I saw fit. Second, I explained that I didn't want to be tied down to the office from nine-to-five, Monday through Friday. I needed the flexibility to work remotely and work the hours necessary to get the job done well. I knew the weight of responsibility that comes with fundraising, and I didn't need someone looking over my shoulder. The executive director agreed to my terms without reservation. She knew I was capable and more than motivated.

I had one more stipulation, though, and it was a rather large one. I asked the executive director to change the home's philosophy of privacy and promotion. Working with young girls from troubled homes, Golden Girl did not do much of anything in the way of promotion. The place was one of the best-kept secrets in rural West Virginia. Rather than draw attention to their work and the good they were doing in the community, they kept quiet, fearing that shining a spotlight could open the girls up to harm. It wasn't an unreasonable conviction, but I had learned through my previous post that it was unnecessary.

The girls at Golden Girl came from all over West Virginia to the very small town of Ceredo. They were far from home, and they were far from the perpetrators of their abuse. I knew it was possible to maintain privacy and get the word out about the home, but I would need permission to reimagine Golden Girl's approach to promotion. Thankfully, the home's leadership agreed it was time to make a change. They were desperate to do so; at the time, the home was struggling to make ends meet.

When I came on board, I wasn't quite sure where to start. But I did know one thing: If I was going to help save Golden Girl, I would need to shout from the rooftops. I would need to tell everyone about the amazing work the home was doing. The time for keeping quiet was over. I had learned years earlier that one of the best ways to promote a nonprofit was to network, so I joined Business Network International (BNI).

The way BNI works in every region is each member represents a single business sector, and no sector can be represented more than once. So, there was someone from the banking industry, another from the insurance world, one from the automotive sector—you get the idea. When I looked into joining, I discovered there was no one representing the nonprofit space, so I signed up to fill that gap.

You may be thinking, *A nonprofit organization isn't a business.* In one sense, you're right. Golden Girl isn't looking to make money for shareholders, and our primary objective isn't turning a profit. Once our obligations are met, all of the extra money we take in (if there is any) is directed back into the home. Our goal is to provide the best living and learning experience for the girls who have been entrusted to us. But to do that, we need to bring in as much money as possible. So, in that sense, Golden Girl is very much like a business, except that, in our case, funding is tied to life transformation. That's our return on investment.

It made a lot of sense for me, as a representative of a nonprofit, to be involved in a business networking group. Because BNI is a noncompetitive group with only one representative from each business sector, everyone involved is there for the benefit of everyone else. Through connection, we help each other grow our businesses. For example, a short while ago, I looked up my "input" into the group—the dollar value of all the referrals I've given to others over the years. I was surprised to discover my help has been worth a whopping $1.3 million. That's just from me helping spread the word about my BNI friends' businesses and services. This works both ways, of course. I have been given many great tips and referrals that have helped me fund projects for Golden Girl.

One of those referrals I told you about in chapter two. I was put in touch with the Tri-State Landscaping Association through a BNI connection, and as you may recall, a phone call led to a visit and a complete overhaul of the outdoor facilities on our campus. The head of the association was looking for a nonprofit to donate to, but he would have certainly chosen another charity had he not been steered my way by a mutual friend. That is the power of networking. It's impossible to know what you're missing out on if you're not doing it every chance you get!

During the more than sixteen years I've spent as a member of BNI, I've learned a lot. One of the most important lessons is one of the simplest: a poverty mentality works against you at every turn. What is a poverty mentality? It's a mentality that says there's only so much money to go around. It's as though funding is a pie with only so many slices, so you have to hurry to make sure you get some. It's a mindset that sees other nonprofits as competitors when the truth is that every good cause is helping make the community a better place.

By nature, I'm a very competitive person, so I'm inclined to chase after my fundraising goals with abandon and to view other fundraising efforts as competition. Through BNI, I saw firsthand how it is better to give than to receive, and to live with an abundance mentality. In reality, when everyone is looking for opportunities to help everyone else, there are more avenues for success. Instead of feeling like I was on my own to fund projects and meet the home's budget, I knew everyone in my network was on my team, ready and available to help however they could. Once you know where to look, there is enough funding for every worthy cause. Someone else's success does not require your failure or vice versa.

Fundraising doesn't have to feel like there's a weight on your back at all times. Instead, it can be more like an adventure. I like to think that my job is a bit like being a detective: I'm always looking for clues, trying to make connections to solve the puzzle that will achieve our financial goals. Over time, I've developed a bit of a sixth sense, seeing every interaction as an opportunity to uncover more clues.

Several years ago, I was at one of my son's high school golf tournaments. My husband couldn't make it that day, so I was by myself. I was riding in a golf cart with another parent, and we were making the usual small talk, which is another way of saying I was networking. I asked him what he did for a living, and he told me he worked for a local coal producer. My fundraising radar went off. I knew that, oftentimes, corporations have foundations that donate to nonprofits in the community. I asked my new friend if his company had such a foundation. He thought for a moment and said, "You know, I'm not sure if we do." But I had told him about Golden Girl, and he wanted to see if there might be some way he could help. He gave me his business card and told me to follow up with him in a few days.

By now, you probably know where this story is going. I followed up with my golf cart companion the next week, and he told me that his company did have a foundation. He gave me the name and email address of a woman who might be able to help me secure a donation for the home. An email led to a phone call and a grant application, and in a few weeks, the foundation donated a brand-new, fifteen-passenger van to Golden Girl—a vehicle we desperately needed at the time.

As I said, many large corporations have a charitable foundation, but most employees, even executives, don't know much about them. That's why it's always a good idea to ask and follow up. I realize that asking about foundation money may be uncomfortable at first, but companies set up foundations because they help ease their tax burden while giving back to the community. They'd rather their money go directly to a cause they believe in than end up with Uncle Sam. Plus, their donations are good publicity for the company. Giving money, or a new van, to a worthy organization is a great public relations move. All that to say, corporations are looking for places to donate money. When you ask, you're not pestering them; you're helping them.

But I do have one word of caution. It's not always clear how large a donation a foundation may be considering, so ask about the average size of their donations. That allows them to steer you in the right direction, and it allows you to apply for something appropriate. (I wouldn't have asked the coal company for a van had they told me they normally only donate a few thousand dollars.)

Sometimes, to help foundations with their public relations, I'll invite them to Golden Girl to present the check or the van or whatever it is they've donated. Or if they've helped with a building project, I'll hold a ribbon-cutting ceremony and invite them to participate as honored guests. These are small ways to show my appreciation, and they provide foundations with great photo opportunities. On occasion, I've written press releases to help get the word out about the good a corporation has done to help our cause. Like I said before, giving is better than receiving, so I'm happy to give back in any way I can.

Whenever a new building project gets underway, I make sure we hold a groundbreaking ceremony. It's a way of marking our fundraising progress, even as much of the physical work is left to be done. Just as it is with a ribbon-cutting event at the completion of a project, the groundbreaking ceremony, complete with hardhats and shovels, is a lot of fun—and it's a great way to show my gratitude to generous donors. I also use these special events to shine a light on the work of Golden Girl.

There was one groundbreaking ceremony we were planning several years back, and I knew the local press would be there, so I spent a few hundred dollars and bought a large banner with the Golden Girl logo emblazoned on it. I also had the home's website and my cell phone number included, just in case someone wanted to find out more about the home or become a donor. At the time, I decided to not make the banner event-specific; I figured we might be able to get more use out of it if I kept things simple. It was a good thing I did because a friend of mine who happened to manage the nearby Big Sandy Superstore Arena (now the Mountain Health Arena) saw the banner and offered to place it in the arena for free.

So, there it was—our banner—hanging up during packed-out concerts and conventions, letting people know there was a special place nearby, helping troubled girls. And it worked! Within a few days, people began calling me. One of those callers was a man named Bart Andrews, a retired but resourceful businessman who had seen the banner and was curious about Golden Girl. He said he was looking for something local in which to invest a bit of his charitable giving. I told him all about the home, and I invited Bart and his wife, Doris, to the campus for a tour.

Bart and Doris loved the home, and Bart gave me a fairly substantial gift a short time after their visit. He also told me he wanted to set up a scholarship fund for the girls through Marshall University. Sadly, it wasn't long after that Bart died of a sudden heart attack; however, to this day, Doris remains a wonderful friend of Golden Girl. She's at our Derby Brunch every year, and she takes a special interest in the girls who are getting ready to leave for college. Thanks to the scholarship fund she and Barth set up years ago, any girl attending Marshall University has all of her ancillary costs covered.

The Andrews have been such a blessing to the young women at Golden Girl, but I have to remind myself that I would not have connected with them if not for two things. First, I had that banner. To be sure, it was a gift to be able to display it in the arena free of charge, but if I had never had it made for the groundbreaking ceremony, there would have been no banner to hang. I learned that even if it costs a little bit of money, publicity is always worth it in the long run. Second, I put my cell phone number on the banner, and I answered every call. Promotion isn't only about getting the word out; it's always about being available when people respond.

That wasn't the end of the banner. When it came time for the Women's Luncheon and Expo to be held at the arena, I pledged some money to become a sponsor. The event is always organized by local radio station KEE 100 FM, so as part of my sponsorship agreement, Golden Girl received several radio spots. Plus, I had a booth at the expo. I hung my banner once again, held a raffle, and my assistant Tanya and I collected lots and lots of new contacts. Afterward, we went through every piece of paper and followed up with people, one of which led to a $15,000 gift.

The radio spots were a wonderful way to reach new people in the area we might not otherwise get a chance to meet. Speaking of radio, it's important to know that local radio and television stations are required by law to commit a certain amount of airtime to public service announcements. Over the years, I've discovered that if I call a station and tell the manager

I'd like to do a PSA about Golden Girl, they're more than happy to oblige. And the wonderful thing is, it costs nothing.

Working with radio and television stations is also a wonderful way to network. Years ago, I met Mike Kirtner of Kindred Communications, and today I count him as a friend. Mike heard about what we were doing at Golden Girl and decided he wanted to help in any way he could. We now regularly trade airtime for tickets to our events. I get to tell people about our mission and how they can get involved, and Mike gets to give away a few tickets to his listeners, bringing even more exposure to the work we're doing.

Depending on the size of your nonprofit, you may not have thought about broadcast media as a promotion tactic, but remember, you are doing good work in your community, and local radio and television outlets want to help spread the word. Take advantage of the opportunities you have.

I realize it may seem like the lesson here is that you need to find yourself a big ole magical banner that will take on a life of its own, become a staple in your community, and garner plenty of new contacts and donations. But the banner was just a simple tool we used for a season. The real lesson I've learned over the years is to take advantage of every free and reasonably priced promotional opportunity available. That may start by adjusting your mindset. I've known many development professionals who assume paid promotion is only for the business sector. But remember, the smartest nonprofits think like businesses. For these organizations, fundraising is no different than being business savvy. They have learned where the money is, what the market demands, and how to get their product in front of the right people at the right time.

Too often, development feels like begging for money, as though nonprofits should be competing for the leftovers. But, as it is with so many aspects of development, success often comes down to having the right perspective. If the cause is a good and worthy one, fundraising is more like extending an invitation. You've discovered something truly worthwhile, and you're offering people the chance to get in on it.

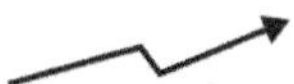

Before we close out this chapter on promotions, there are two more avenues I want to tell you about, and they're so important that I had to save them for last. The first is this: you must have a newsletter.

In a world where everyone has a phone in their pocket and we're all on social media, it may seem like printed newsletters are a thing of the past. But I haven't given up on them just yet. That's because a newsletter allows you to tell your stories without competing with other blurbs on a perpetually scrolling newsfeed. A newsletter is an opportunity to spread the word about the awesome work your organization is doing with everyone in your database. They give you the chance to share your successes with people who care and to let them know about upcoming events, all without distraction.

I'm not suggesting you abandon social media. Every organization needs to figure out the right blend of channels for their communication strategy. But I do suggest you consider putting out two to four newsletters each year. I've found that two is just about right for Golden Girl. In the spring, I highlight the Derby Brunch and share success stories about girls who are set to graduate high school. Then, in the fall, I point ahead to Christmas and invite donors to get involved in what we're planning at the home. And of course, in each issue, I write about current projects, needs, and goals we're hoping to reach.

With a newsletter, I can reach everyone on our list. It's more personal than an email, and it doesn't depend on the donors finding us. For the people who are uniquely invested in the work we're doing, our newsletters are like a letter in the mail from a friend, reminding them why they decided to contribute to the work of Golden Girl in the first place and keeping them engaged for the next season.

Finally, the best type of promotion is also the most rewarding—word of mouth. You've probably heard the saying, "It takes a lifetime to build a reputation but a moment to destroy one." It's true, so make sure people have nothing but good things to say about your nonprofit. If people love what you do, they'll pass it on. Personal references and connections go a lot further than any banner or radio PSA ever will.

Years ago, one of our program's graduates had a job working at a local Arby's restaurant. The owner of the franchise gave money to local charities each year, and he let his employees help choose which ones. Well, our graduate spoke up and said she wanted to give back to Golden Girl. She gave the store manager my contact information, and she reached out to me and told me the restaurant would like to donate to the home. That was one of the most rewarding donations the home has ever received, not because of the dollar amount but because it came through someone who was transformed through the work we do. I couldn't have asked for a better endorsement.

I told the manager that I'd be happy to come to the restaurant so they could do a check presentation. As I said before, institutional donors like check presentations and ribbon-cutting ceremonies because they make for good PR. She agreed, and I went down for the photo op. That's when I discovered the owner of the restaurant didn't merely own one Arby's; he owned all the other Arby's in the state of West Virginia and a few others in other states. The personal connection I made that day cemented a new relationship. Over the years, the owner of these restaurants has graciously donated to Golden Girl time and time again—everything from new school clothes to a new van.

These days, it seems like a lot of people are quick to complain and slow to compliment, but if your nonprofit gives people something to feel good about, they'll talk about it. And it's that kind of word of mouth that opens doors—doors you never knew existed.

Somewhere along the way, many of us believed the lie that a nonprofit doesn't need to be as vocal as a for-profit brand. Promotions, we were told, were for marketing teams to generate sales. But nonprofits and charities have cause to be the most vocal. In the case of Golden Girl, our work transforms lives. That's worth shouting about!

So, go ahead. Buy the banner. Schedule the ribbon cutting. Put that newsletter together. Call a local radio station and ask to record a PSA. The world is waiting to hear from you.

Unless you spend your days at home alone, you probably utter the simple phrase, "Thank you," dozens of times each day. When the barista hands you a hazelnut latté, "Thank you!" When the stranger walking in front of you holds the door open, "Thank you!" When your coworker compliments your outfit, "Thank you!"

"Thank you" is all around us. We offer it. We receive it. But rarely do we stop to think about its power. And yet, we know there's something deeply wrong with a person who never thanks others. That's because, while the words *thank you* don't have magical powers, they convey something nearly magical—honor. Thanking someone is a way of acknowledging their kindness, their presence, and their humanity. It's one of the simple graces we extend to one another, and it is an essential part of fundraising. I often tell other development professionals, "Even if you don't do anything else, make sure you say, 'Thank you!'"

Of course, not every thank you looks the same. And that's good. As much as possible, every offering of thanks should be as unique as the individual you're thanking. With that in mind, I generally think about thank you in three categories—handwritten notes, personalized gifts, and legacy gifts.

Years ago, I was attending an event at the Lilly Family School of Philanthropy at Indiana University, and I asked my classmates a simple question: "How many times have you received a handwritten note in response to a financial gift you gave?" I looked around the room, and very few people raised their hands. But there was a time when thank you cards were standard operating procedure. It would have been unthinkable to receive a gift and not offer a personal note of thanks. But today life moves at the speed of 5G downloads and one-click shopping. Writing handwritten notes has become something of a lost art. Even so, in the world of fundraising, it remains a powerful tool.

For many years now, I've made it a nonnegotiable at Golden Girl. When someone donates to our home —no matter how big or small—I write a personal note to thank them. These notes aren't long, but they are personal. With each one, I try to remember some special details about their gift or the interactions we've had. I might ask them about their kids or how their recent trip abroad went. A little touch like that lets the donor know they're not just a number on the balance sheet; they're part of the work we're doing. I know there are a million ministries, causes, and nonprofits to which they could have sent their hard-earned money, but they chose to share with us. That *is* special, so I want them to know they, too, are special.

Even if your organization is large and you receive

thousands upon thousands of donations each year, I recommend taking the time to send a handwritten note to every single donor. At first, that might seem like a lot of extra work, but it can be divvied up among your staff. Also, most new database systems will allow you to track details of your interactions with donors, so when it comes time to write those personal cards, you'll be able to recall something unique about each one.

A handwritten note stands out, where a form letter or a printed receipt falls flat. It's my way of saying, "I see you, and I want to honor you!" What I've discovered over the years is that these little notes mean a lot to people. Those who receive them form a special attachment to Golden Girl. They stay invested in the work we're doing, and they are tuned in when I send out a newsletter or hold an event. And frankly, it's the right thing to do, no matter how busy life gets.

One step up from a handwritten note is a personalized gift. I don't have a hard and fast rule about when I send someone a small gift to say thank you, but I enjoy honoring larger and long-term donors with a little something special from time to time. And honestly, I love that part of my job. It is a lot of fun to bless people with unexpected gifts!

They aren't expensive gestures; they're small, very reasonably priced gifts. For example, there's a donor who has been generous over the years, and I happen to know he loves to play golf. So, I ordered him a set of golf balls with his name on them. He loved the gift— and now he thinks of Golden Girl whenever he tees off with one.

Another time, I had my daughter, who's an artist,

paint a beautiful tree without any leaves. Then I bought ink pads in lots of fun, bright colors and had all the girls at the home leave a thumbprint on the tree and sign their names. Then I had the beautiful tree with all of those thumbprint leaves framed. I gave it to one of the state agencies that helped facilitate a grant for Golden Girl. They loved it, and they hung it in their lobby. Years later, it's still the first thing you see when you walk into their office.

The key to a great gift is that it needs to be personal, either something that will speak to the life of the donor who's going to receive it or something special from your organization. Again, these gifts don't have to be expensive. The point is the gesture and the thought behind it—the honor that is bestowed—not the dollar value of the gift.

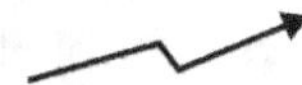

Finally, there's the legacy gift. Typically, these are rare and should be reserved for very special donors. Again, there's no rule about when to give someone a legacy gift as a thank you; it's about honoring someone who has made a unique contribution to your organization. And there's nothing quite like the indelible mark a legacy gift offers.

On the second floor of the Golden Minds Center for Learning and Development is the Laurie Fox Legacy Tea Room. As I mentioned earlier, this space is used for special events, etiquette training, and unique learning opportunities at Golden Girl. It's named for Laurie Fox, a wonderful, deeply invested donor who passed away a few years ago. As you enter the room, a picture of Laurie greets you along with a sign that says Laurie's Tea Room. Against one wall is an antique

China cabinet filled with Laurie's China, a gift from her husband, David, who's still very involved with the home.

Laurie was a mentor to the girls, and I know she would have been right at home, sitting down to tea with them in the tea room. It seemed fitting that her memory fills that space as an ongoing testimony to her kindness and devotion to the work of Golden Girl. At the ribbon cutting, I asked David to speak. I wanted to make sure Laurie's legacy was honored appropriately and that he knew just how much we loved her.

Legacy gifts are unique and powerful and should be used sparingly. They're not for everyone, but even when you decide to give one of your most deserving partners a legacy gift, it may not be the best idea. Some donors like recognition; others prefer to remain anonymous and stay behind the scenes. Before you choose to esteem someone publicly with a legacy gift, make sure they are comfortable receiving such an honor.

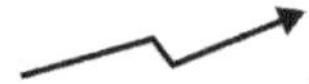

In addition to the three main categories above, there is also the thank you phone call. At Golden Girl, we hold regular thank-a-thons, where our staff joins forces to call every single donor in our database to thank them personally. If the person answers the phone, we get the opportunity to chat with them for a minute, thank them for their gift to the home, and answer any questions they may have. If they don't answer, we leave them a sweet voicemail message of thanks. Either way, it's a small but personal touch that lets our friends know we are grateful for their partnership in the work we're doing.

But I do have a few words of caution when it comes to phone calls. A phone call is not a substitute for a handwritten note. In our disposable world, a handwritten note simply conveys gratitude in a way a phone call rarely can. In addition, people don't answer the phone the way they once did, so making a personal connection has become more difficult. That said, phone calls do not hurt, so if you have the bandwidth as an organization, a phone campaign is an excellent way to add an extra thank you to your development strategy.

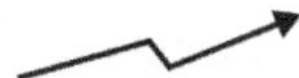

"Thank you!" is more than something you say; it's an attitude that ought to permeate everything we do as development professionals. Without the generous support of donors, volunteers, and contributors, our efforts would be for nothing. Fundraising is never a solo endeavor. It depends on lots of people stepping forward and saying, "Yes! Count me in!" At the heart of all great fundraising is a spirit of gratitude and an atmosphere of honor.

Most of us don't spend much time thinking about honor. It's one of those values that's either embedded in everyday life or it isn't. Oftentimes, it only comes up when we feel *dishonored*. In development, a culture of honor can make or break your fundraising strategy. If you fail to honor the people you serve and the people who give generously, the best events, the most polished newsletters, and the greatest promotions won't mean a thing.

You may be wondering, "What exactly does a culture of honor look like?" To illustrate, I want to tell you about an experience we had at Golden Girl not too long ago. It's a bit extreme—not the sort of thing that happens to us every day—but it shows what a thankful spirit and a culture of honor look like when blown up beyond normal proportions.

It all started with a text from my friend Alys Smith —the first lady of Marshall University. Alys is married to Brad Smith, the former CEO of Intuit, the company that created TurboTax, QuickBooks, and Mint financial software. He's now the president of Marshall. Alys and Brad are generous donors to many worthy causes, especially to organizations in their backyard in West Virginia. They also have many influential and generous friends. That's actually why Alys texted me. She wanted to let me know that Sheryl Sandberg was coming for a visit to the area and that she was planning on making a stop at Golden Girl.

Even if you don't know the name Sheryl Sandberg, you've probably been impacted by her work. She's been a senior employee at Google and World Bank, and she was chief of staff to the secretary of the treasury in Bill Clinton's White House. Most recently she was chief operating officer at Meta Platforms, formerly known as Facebook. To say she's an important business leader in the United States would be an understatement. In 2012, *Time* magazine listed Sandberg as one of the "Top 100: Most Influential People in the World." In 2021, she was number eight on *Fortune*'s list of the "Most Powerful Women in Business." And she was coming to our small town in just a few weeks.

Now, I'm not one to be wowed by money, fame, or success. I wasn't thinking about potential donations or what an influential businesswoman could do for our little nonprofit. I simply recognized that Sheryl is an incredibly busy person and that there are many demands on her time and attention. But she had heard about the mission of Golden Girl, and she planned to set aside a small portion of her quick trip to West Virginia to visit us in person. That gesture was worthy of honor; her visit was deserving of our full attention.

Right away, I got to work. The first thing I wanted to do was make sure the girls took full advantage of the opportunity. I wanted them to get to know and appreciate our special guest. Sheryl had written a book called *Lean In*, about how women can find success in business and life. I listened to the whole thing on audiobook in just a few days, and then I ordered copies for all of our older girls. Before Sheryl arrived, I wanted them to know a bit about her story and how she approached life.

Obviously, not everyone you'll meet will have their own book you can read to find out about them. But the principle holds true: One of the very best ways to honor someone and show you appreciate them is to find out who they are, what motivates them, and where they're hoping to go in life. So, ask questions, do a bit of research, and step forward with curiosity. It can be easy for development professionals to get so focused on their cause that they forget to have a two-way conversation. But every person you interact with has a story. As you share the story of your organization, make time for your donors to tell you a bit about their journey.

Because Sheryl travels with security detail and because she had many stops to make during her visit to West Virginia, we didn't know exactly when she'd be arriving. That meant it was difficult for us to prepare in advance. I wanted to have food and refreshments ready, but without knowing when Sheryl and her crew would be joining us, it was difficult to plan. (Her crew included her husband, Tom Bernthal, her children, members of her extended family, Alys and Brad Smith, and security personnel.) Would it be a late brunch? Or perhaps lunch or a mid-afternoon snack? The best we could do was remain flexible. I tried to keep in rhythm with her schedule, even though that meant being unsettled for a couple of days. Again, I realize Sheryl's visit was atypical, but the principle can be applied to every guest you welcome: do your best to anticipate their needs so you can alleviate stress from their life, not add to it.

As it turned out, Sheryl and company didn't have enough time in their schedule for any sort of refreshments, so meal preparation wasn't required. When I found out their agenda was compressed, I wondered if Sheryl would seem rushed and overwhelmed. But when she arrived, I discovered she was anything but stressed. In all those years of managing the portfolios of large corporations, she had learned to take things in stride. I learned from her book that she was a woman in charge of her environment. She had her priorities in line and made herself available to people at the moment in which she was living. If there was one attribute that caught my attention when I met Sheryl, it was this—she was kind. You might assume that a fabulously successful businesswoman would be a bit out of touch with everyday people, but Sheryl was genuinely interested in our work at Golden Girl.

I took Sheryl and our other guests on a tour of one of our campus houses and introduced her to several of the girls. The girls had an opportunity to ask Sheryl about *Lean In*, then I took everyone to the Golden Minds Center for Learning and Development. I showed off our boutique and our learning center and answered questions about our program for high school girls and those who had graduated to independent living.

Something Alys had told me days earlier lingered in my brain, and I wanted to find a way to make the visit truly powerful. I knew Sheryl felt for the girls in our program, and Alys had told me how she was always looking for opportunities to help her children grow in generosity and kindness. So, while in Laurie's Tea Room, I asked everyone to have a seat. I had placed a card and a pen at every place setting, and I invited our guests to write short notes of encouragement to the girls at our home. A couple of Sheryl's children were in grade school, and a couple more were in high school. Alys and Brad were there, with Sheryl's and Tom's parents. Every generation was represented in the room that day, and it was an activity for all ages. And I could see they truly enjoyed having the opportunity to bless our girls with a kind word. It was probably the most meaningful few minutes of their entire visit.

My goal in including that small activity at the close of our time together was to allow Sheryl, and especially her children, to leave behind a little bit of inspiration. It was an invitation to speak into the lives of our girls. I hoped that both our girls and Sheryl's children would see that the gap between Silicon Valley and the hills of Appalachia isn't that big after all. And I wanted to honor Sheryl's desire to raise her kids to help and encourage other people.

Oftentimes, the best way to honor someone is to invite them to serve. Think about your own life for a moment. When you have people over to your house for a dinner party, who comes into the kitchen to help you out? Your closest friends, right? Asking someone to help out is a way of inviting them to step closer.

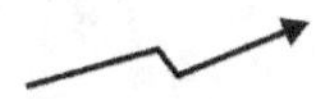

If you step outside and stare at the sun for any length of time, you'll soon find you can't see anything else. At best, spots will fill your field of vision, and at worst, you'll do permanent damage to your eyes. You'll probably stumble and fall or walk into danger. But if you avoid looking directly at the sun and instead look at the world around you by the sun's light, you'll see clearly to know where to step.

Too many development professionals fall into the trap of staring directly at their financial goals for so long that they become blind to everything else. They become fixated and miss what's right in front of them. Money is just a tool, after all, and when we understand that fundraising is just a means to bring our passions to life, we are set free to see the people around us as men and women worthy of honor. That's what cultivates an atmosphere of thankfulness, and it shapes everything about our efforts.

You may not have one of the world's most influential businesswomen coming to visit, but you interact with people every day. Every single one of them is worthy of honor. Say thank you when someone makes a donation or pledges their time. Write a note. Send a gift. But don't forget to say thank you in advance by honoring people as soon as they step into your life. Learn about their background and their interests. Be hospitable. Invite them to step closer. It can make all the difference in the world.

CHAPTER EIGHT

THIRTEEN STORIES, FIFTY MILLION DOLLARS, AND NO TURNING BACK

A long Sixth Avenue in downtown Huntington, West Virginia, there's an old hotel. Just shy of one hundred years old at the time of this writing, the Prichard has seen a lot of life. At one point, with its three hundred luxuriously appointed guest rooms, it was the nicest place in town to stay. Two radio stations once called the Prichard home. Exclusive events were held in the hotel's ballroom, and the restaurant served some of the best meals in West Virginia. Gene Autry once stayed there, as did John F. Kennedy and his family during his 1960 presidential campaign.

But all of that was a long time ago. Over the past few decades, the Prichard has fallen into disrepair. In the 1970s, the once stately hotel became a mixed-use apartment and office building. In the 2000s, drug use was rampant, and crime surged. The glimmer of days gone by had all but dulled. By 2015, the Prichard was lifeless and decaying—that is until a few years ago when Pastor Chuck Lawrence of Christ Temple Church became convinced that something had to be done with the property. The church has a long track record of identifying needs in the community and finding ways to meet those needs. The Prichard itself was in need. Without a new vision for the building, it would continue to decay, and continue to stand as a monument to brokenness and loss—a reminder that things are not as they should be. That's when Pastor Chuck asked me to get involved and when my life was overtaken by all things Prichard Hotel. Chuck didn't know exactly what needed to be done to rehabilitate the Prichard; he only knew *something* had to change, and he wanted to be a part of it. Seeing that Pastor Chuck was all in, so was I.

I mentioned at the start of this book that I had undertaken a $50.8 million fundraising project. As we began talking about renovating the Prichard, I didn't know what it would cost, but slowly and steadily, as I began exploring all that would be needed to bring the building back to life, the price tag became clear. It's by far the biggest venture I've ever been a part of. Over the past five years, I've had many sleepless nights. On more than one occasion, I've thought about giving up. I've wondered if all my efforts were for nothing—if what we were attempting was even possible. But when I would run into a dead end, I would pause and look around, do a bit of investigating, and find a way to take a few steps further. That's how this fundraising project came along—bit by bit, struggle by struggle, discovery by discovery.

To be completely honest with you—and hopefully, by this point, you know I try to never sugarcoat anything—I didn't know what I was doing when I started. I'd never tried to manage a building project as big as the Prichard. I'd never had to raise a sum that had so many zeros on the end. I wish I could tell you that I simply followed an easy-to-use guide to get the effort across the finish line, but that's not how it happened. I stumbled through for several years, I asked for help, and more than once I had to put my detective hat on and find the next clue.

Though the stakes were certainly higher, the process was the same as it was with other projects I've managed. **Passion** was essential. I don't know how I could have continued if I didn't believe strongly in what we were doing. **Building relationships** was key as well. I met lots of new people because of the Prichard, and I needed to—there was no way I could have done it on my own. **Asking questions** was vital. Over the years, I've learned the best thing to do when you don't know what you should be doing is to find someone who's traveled the same road already, request to meet with them, and ask questions. Most people are more than willing to help—if they know what information you need.

But I'm getting ahead of myself…

For years, the thirteen-story Prichard Hotel loomed over downtown Huntington, almost mocking anyone who longed to see the building transformed. Attempts had been made of course. In 2015, Polan Realty purchased the building and tried to turn it into a nonprofit drug rehabilitation facility. The idea was simple: The lower floors could be used for treatment while the apartments above could serve as living quarters for those who struggled with addiction. Not only would such a plan have revitalized the old Prichard, but it would have served people in desperate need, people who often fall through the cracks of society. However, it was not to be.

When the time came to inspect the building—to see what was needed to bring it up to current building standards and regulations—the structural and environmental problems began to mount. Before long, Shane Polan and his team had no choice but to abandon their vision.

A few years passed, and another vision was born—by my husband, Bobby. Knowing that our pastor had asked me to help with an effort to breathe new life into the old Prichard Hotel, he suggested transforming the building into a senior living center, something the community could use but that could also pay for itself over time.

Pastor Chuck and the small team at Christ Temple Church were enthusiastic about the idea. And so, the first thing I did was form a nonprofit. It would be the backbone of our fundraising efforts and everything would flow through it, as a separate entity from the church. As a team—Jamie Lawrence, Bobby Thomas, Randy Saunders, Brenda Landers, Rocky Adkins, and me—we dubbed it the Cornerstone Community Development Corporation.

In ancient times, the cornerstone of a building was the first stone laid, and its purpose was to ensure that all the other stones were level and straight. The New Testament tells us Jesus is the cornerstone of the church (Ephesians 2:20). This nonprofit would be our "first stone," so to speak, but we also wanted a constant reminder that, ultimately, our work would be dedicated to the Lord as a way to love our neighbors. That wasn't to give it a religious tone, of course; it was to serve as a reminder that our motivation is to bless others—not just the seniors who will one day live in the restored

Prichard but the entire community, who would have something new downtown to be proud of.

A nonprofit entity is the foundation of any large building project. Through the corporation, a board oversees the work, bylaws regulate the conduct of the organization, and legal status is established. Cornerstone cemented our goals for the Prichard so anyone who wanted to partner with our team could know their money (or their time or expertise) would serve the original vision we had set forth. In a sense, it bound us to our plans.

In those early days of Cornerstone, while we were still assessing all the Prichard would need for its new shot at life, I was a bit overwhelmed. I didn't know how we would do what seemed impossible, but somehow the creation of Cornerstone helped me set our dreams in reality. I remember reading in the Bible that King Solomon "succeeded in carrying out all he had in mind to do" (2 Chronicles 7:11), and I tried to picture myself at the end of the project being able to say the same about our team. I wanted us to succeed in carrying out all we had in mind to do. Cornerstone gave me the space to figure out how I could get there.

Even though there was a lot I didn't know, from the beginning we needed to have a realistic budget. That meant anticipating all of the costs we would certainly incur and many more that we didn't anticipate. At no point was the budget etched in stone because the more we dug in, the more we learned what would be needed; however, it was a real budget because even the surprises were somewhere on my balance sheet.

As the months and years rolled by, I discovered more and more of what I didn't know about funding a project that large. If you're someone who likes to know the path you must take all that time, what I'm about to tell you may make you uncomfortable. There were three truths I had to keep coming back to.

Above all, **I had to remember to be myself**. This meant not pretending I was someone I was not. There is a temptation when you step into something new—to "fake it till you make it." That's even offered as sage advice by leadership gurus these days. And to some extent, it's helpful. It allows a person to work with confidence until he or she figures things out. But it can also hinder that person from growing. I found that in leading the team at Christ Temple and working through Cornerstone to refurbish the Prichard, I learned more and navigated unknown waters faster and more confidently by being honest with myself and others. That leads me to the next truth I learned.

Ask Questions. I can't emphasize how important it is to ask questions. I've mentioned this necessary truth of fundraising already, but it bears repeating. Every development project is different, so no matter how experienced you may be, you will never have all the answers. You will never know all there is to know, and the only way to grow and meet your goals is to ask questions. The easiest way to stall your fundraising efforts is to stop talking. The more connections you make, the more experts you'll have at your disposal. When you do have questions, you'll have the right person to ask somewhere in your list of contacts.

At one point, I took all the paperwork that was required for the various stages of permitting, licensing, contracting, etc., and stacked it up in one big pile. It was taller than I was. If I had seen that before I started, it would have frightened me—maybe even to the point of stepping away from the Prichard—but every document had a purpose, and every single one required knowledge on my part. I didn't have all that knowledge when I started fundraising. Building relationships and asking questions was the only way I could get through it all.

Early on, I reached out to a contact I had made when I was working on the apartment project for Golden Girl. George Carico at West Virginia Brownfields Assistance Center at Marshall University had helped me navigate the environmental issue when we discovered our potential property had gas tanks buried underground. Knowing the Prichard was likely to have environmental problems, given its age and sordid history, I contacted George again. He told me about an important training seminar where I could learn more about the environmental regulations in play and the path I would need to take. I could also ask lots and lots of questions.

Though it required a two-hour drive each way, attending the training turned out to be one of the best decisions I made. I found out I could apply for a federal grant that would help bring the Prichard up to code, concerning the EPA's current standards. I applied, and Cornerstone was awarded a $500,000 grant. I also discovered a State of West Virginia grant that replaced many (but not all) of the old windows in the building. It was a big step forward, and it was all due to me picking up the phone and asking a simple question.

Finally, **I had to learn to admit my weaknesses**. When you're the "development expert," people tend to look to you for all the answers. They also think the work is somehow easier for you since it's your profession. But no single person knows everything, and no single person can carry all the weight. Fifty million dollars is too much for one person to raise on their own. Learning what's needed to legally, effi-

ciently, and safely plan for the renovation of a dilapidated thirteen-story hotel is a job for many, many
people. Early on, I had to admit to myself and my
team that I needed help.

Full disclosure: I didn't carve out enough time for
myself as I worked on the Prichard. There were times
when I let the work consume my days and nights, my
weekends, and my off-hours. I didn't guard my family
time the way I should have. I didn't care for myself the
way I should have. As I've already mentioned, there
were many sleepless nights when I could do nothing
but think through all that needed to be done to reach
the next milestone on the project. My mind was so
consumed with the Prichard that other important
things fell to the wayside. I suppose that is the
dangerous flipside of passion. I wasn't able to let go
when I needed to. I'm admitting this to you now in the
name of knowing my weaknesses. I'm not proud of it,
but it is what it is.

Whatever your project is, I hope you will build
boundaries better than I was able to do. Don't get me
wrong. No effort the size of the Prichard can be made
with a part-time mindset; however, it shouldn't and
doesn't have to take over every aspect of your life.
Invite someone to hold you accountable. Surround
yourself with people who will be honest with you. And
above all, be honest with yourself. That means sched-
uling time to make sure you are caring for yourself—
emotionally, physically, mentally, and spiritually.
Remember, it's not a win for anyone if the project rises
but you fall to the ground, exhausted and depleted.

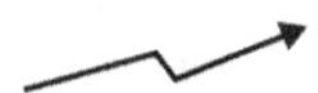

As I mentioned earlier, Polan Realty owned the Prichard when we first got started. While Shane Polan was happy to assist in our plans to bring the hotel back to life, we knew that to make headway, Cornerstone would need full site control. That meant buying the property from Polan. Thankfully, there was a donor lined up to buy the hotel through Cornerstone.

For $1 million, the historic building transferred hands. I remember sitting in the lawyer's office for the closing and holding the check. At that moment, the weight of what we were trying to do hit me—and if it hadn't, the way the attorney quickly took the check from me would have! Having control of the property was important because donors, investors, and partners need to know their money is going to something real, something we have the authority to work on. While I knew it was the right move, there was something about the transaction that made me sick to my stomach. One million dollars was already on the line, and I had agreed to lead the charge to raise more than fifty times that amount. There would be no turning back, no giving up if we encountered obstacles. For better or worse, I would be in it for the long haul, and there was so much about the Prichard we had yet to discover.

With other building projects, I had worked with for-profit companies and their donors and sponsors, but I had never entered into a full partnership with one. With the Prichard, however, I learned that to raise the necessary funding and provide for a life beyond the construction, I needed to find someone who could help me with the heavy lifting, someone who could take me down avenues ordinarily closed to nonprofits. And I needed someone who would invest in the future of the Prichard when my work was over and done.

Our vision was to turn the Prichard into a senior

living apartment complex with an on-site health center. That would require someone to run the day-to-day operations after the final dollar was raised and the final coat of paint dried. Along the way, we would need access to federal funding, tax credits, and bonds available to for-profit corporations. So, we began our search.

There's no magic formula for finding a good building partner. It's like any other relationship; you have to make sure the partnership will be a good fit for both entities and beneficial for both in the long run. Of course, the most important element in any relationship, business or otherwise, is trust. If there's no trust, there is no relationship. Before anything gets signed and any money exchanges hands, spend some time seeing if trust can be built.

Before we found our corporate partner for the Prichard, there was a firm I spent a good bit of time getting to know. On paper, they were a perfect fit. They knew the senior living market and were eager to join Cornerstone in developing the Prichard and overseeing the day-to-day management of the building's residents and programs. But there was a feeling in my gut I just couldn't shake. Something didn't sit right with me. I've learned that when this happens, the best thing to do is dig in and ask lots and lots of questions. That's just what I did.

I was surprised at how many basic questions about the process that potential partner could not answer. I'm certainly no expert when it comes to tax credits and bonds, but I know enough to know when someone else knows even less! Before long, we walked away from the relationship. I'm thankful I listened to my gut, and I'm grateful nothing had been signed when I realized that particular company was not a good fit for the

Prichard. Honestly, I don't know what I would have done if we had entered into a legal partnership and I had discovered something was wrong. I tell you this only because it is so important to make sure that, on any project, you are aligned with your partners. Trust is everything. If someone alarms you, pay attention.

After that near-miss, we found a new for-profit corporate partner in Winterwood, Inc., a regional property management company that was excited to see the Prichard return to its former glory. Not only that, they had completed over $1 billion in commercial development in the past; a large project like ours was nothing unusual to them. Once again, I asked lots and lots of questions; and the more I asked, the more I grew certain Winterwood was the right business partner.

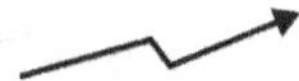

With more than one hundred and forty thousand square feet to renovate and $50.8 million in play, I knew there would be no shortage of surprises and curveballs along the way. I want to tell you about one of them. It is in no way exemplary, as I imagine every large project has shockers and pitfalls; however, I'm detailing this one because it demonstrates there is no way to prepare for every obstacle. All you can do is remain mentally nimble and remind yourself that **for every problem there is a solution, even if it's not immediately apparent**.

As the time was drawing near to close on the Prichard deal, with all the donors and investors and business partners coming together to sign on the dotted line—many, many dotted lines (Have I mentioned how much paperwork there was?)—I was notified there was a problem, and if not remedied quickly, the entire deal would fall through. All the arrangements and agreements, hard work, and long hours I'd put in, would be for nothing.

The parking lot attached to the Prichard was not entirely part of the property. About half of the lot was owned by the building next door, a building that was not part of the deal and had no connection to the historic Prichard. Some of the investors were not willing to put their money down unless the entire parking lot was included in the deal—if there wasn't enough parking for all the seniors who would one day live at the Prichard, it would be difficult to fill all the apartments.

I had one day to see if the owner of the building next door would be willing to sell their property. If so, I would have to find a donor to finance the purchase. And if I could do all that, I would have to have all the paperwork ready to sell the parking lot back to the Prichard at the time of the deal closing. Talk about being stressed out!

I took the challenge on, one piece at a time. The first thing I did was contact the owner of the building next door to the Prichard to see if he would be willing to sell. Although he had a few tenants in the building, he said he was willing to sell the property to Cornerstone. I was elated and told the others on my team the good news. Thankfully, as was with the original purchase of the Prichard, there was a donor ready and willing to purchase the additional property through Cornerstone. It was incredible!

Just hours before, it had appeared to be an impossible problem, but the community came together to make sure the Prichard deal would still happen—on time and in full. I can look back and see the hand of

God in all of it. (Whether others see providence at work is their own business.) There was a narrow path to achieve our goal, and I walked it step by step, believing we could get everything done on time, and it happened.

As amazing as all of that was, here's the most amazing part. Years ago, when Pastor Chuck and others at Christ Temple Church began wondering what might be done with the Prichard property, there was a collective desire to do something to help at-risk youth. As you know, I was once one of those at-risk teenagers. Also, my day job is with the Golden Girl Group Home. I understand the plight of children who come from abusive or neglectful homes. It would be an understatement to say I am concerned about the well-being of these young people. But when we looked at the Prichard and what it would take to revitalize it, it soon became apparent there would need to be a larger revenue source for the ongoing maintenance of the building; the Prichard wouldn't be able to serve young adults aging out of foster care. The numbers just couldn't get us there.

The problem of needing the entire parking lot for the Prichard created a tremendous opportunity, though it certainly didn't seem like one at the time. Corner-stone now had ownership of a new building, and our dream of providing affordable and safe apartments for young people aging out of the state foster care system could become a reality. Plus, having the two buildings side-by-side would create an intergenerational synergy, an intentional community of young and old. When I think about it, I am struck by how the most stressful couple of days in the six-year-long Prichard project turned into something so beautiful, and it was some-thing we never could have planned for. I tell you this because **the greatest challenges you face might become opportunities to do more good than you dared to imagine**.

I spent nearly seven hours in an attorney's office downtown on the day the deal closed. The amount of paper involved was incredible. (I had no idea they even made file folders that big.) But after that long day, with money having changed hands and all the legal documents having been signed, Cornerstone was empowered to move forward with the actual renovations on the Prichard. And while I celebrated like never before as I drove home that day, I knew we needed something more than a legal wrap-up to this part of our journey; we needed a time to celebrate.

On the afternoon of February 6, 2024, people from the community of Huntington and from across the country gathered to take part in the groundbreaking ceremony for the Prichard's renovations. Over the six years I worked to develop the project, more than twenty partner organizations joined the team. On the day of the groundbreaking, there were lots of amazing, wonderful people who came to the site to celebrate with us.

In a large, heated tent, more than one hundred people gathered. It was standing room only, with over one hundred more people waiting outside to get in. A beautiful backdrop of the Prichard in its glory days hung behind the podium for all to see. Gourmet hot chocolates were served. Some stakeholders swung sledgehammers in a mock demolition, while others wore hard hats and shoveled dirt that we had brought in. When you erect a building from scratch, the groundbreaking is the breaking of the ground to commence construction. Since our project involved an existing building, I wanted to make sure the experience of a true groundbreaking would be replicated.

Representatives from Aetna and CVS were there, as both companies were major sponsors of the project. State Senator Bob Plymale was there; he had been a huge supporter of the Prichard renovation from the beginning. My friends, Brad and Alys Smith, were there as well. Brad, as you may recall, is the president of Marshall University. His heart is to develop, serve, and dream big. Somewhere along the way, he caught the vision for the project, so of course, when the decision was made to include a health center in the building, Marshall Health Network stepped in.

The groundbreaking ceremony was a chance to look back on the Prichard's wonderful legacy while also looking ahead to the future, but mostly it was an opportunity to rejoice in all the wonderful ways so many different people came together to bring a dream into reality. A lot of people said it couldn't be done. Others said $50.8 million was simply too much money to raise for a project like this. Naysayers thought there were too many obstacles to overcome. But as we sipped hot chocolate on that brisk February afternoon, there were smiles everywhere. And if you had been there, you would have seen the biggest one on me.

I began this book by saying passion has to be the driving force behind any fundraising project. With all my heart, I believe that's true. But here's the thing about passion: It has the power to take you places you never thought possible. If you believe in a cause with all your heart, mind, and strength, you will not only achieve your goals, but you'll also inspire others around you to join in. And when people across a community come together, their efforts are multiplied. Before long, you'll realize your original goals were too small, and you'll start looking for something bigger. If you keep at it, this will happen time and time again. As the years go by, you'll discover your adventure has taken you to new heights—ones you couldn't even see from the ground when you were just starting.

It's okay to hate fundraising. Just love the cause you're passionate about, and, after a while, it won't feel much like fundraising anymore.

NOTES

INTRODUCTION

1. Rob Webb, "nonprofit Development Staff Turnover: Is It a Crisis or an Old Paradigm We Need to Change?" nonprofit PRO, April 26, 2022, https://www.nonprofitpro.com/post/nonprofit-development-staff-turnover-is-it-a-crisis-or-an-old-paradigm-we-need-to-change/.

1. PASSION IS THE REASON

1. I'm not sure what path you're on at the moment, but I assume you picked up this book to learn more about fundraising (and we will get to that in just a moment). As I share this part of my story, I want you to know it's just that—*my* story. Maybe you're a person of faith, and maybe you're not. Either way, you have a story, and in that story lies your passion. I want you to know this book is for people of every faith or no faith in particular. The principles I outline are not confined to Christianity or any other way of life.

2. NO, REALLY. PASSION IS THE REASON

1. Many names have been changed for privacy.

Nikki Thomas, an award-winning nonprofit executive, has taken organizations with little or no exposure to a solid brand that generates multiple streams of income. Nikki has overcome many obstacles in her life, including homelessness at the age of 16. With a master's degree and more than two decades of experience, she has raised over 100 million dollars through her development career. She has a desire to help charitable organizations of all sizes become prosperous and self-sufficient. Nikki lives in Ohio with her husband of 39 years. Her family includes four children, three grandchildren and a retired racehorse named "Bernie."